MAKING
SENSE
OF EVIL

9 / 11

Eyewitness

Finds

Answers

To Heather —
Triumphant in Christ!
Peg Rankin

MAKING SENSE OF EVIL

9/11
Eyewitness
Finds
Answers

PEG RANKIN

Pleasant Word
A Division of WINEPRESS PUBLISHING

Pleasant Word (a division of WinePress Publishing, PO Box 428, Enumclaw, WA 98022) functions only as book publisher. As such, the ultimate design, content, editorial accuracy, and views expressed or implied in this work are those of the author.

ISBN 1-4141-0763-3
Library of Congress Catalog Card Number: 2006904556

DEDICATION

To my beloved husband,
Lee,
with whom I am one in spirit and in purpose.

ACKNOWLEDGEMENTS

With gratitude to the following individuals:

- Pastor James Loveland for suggesting I write on the topic of evil and for carefully checking my theology and biblical content;

- Barbara Mikuszewski for making valuable contributions as a lay reader;

- Carol Murr for giving the book its title;

- My husband Lee for typing, editing, supporting, and being a source of constant encouragement;

- Family members and friends who prayed that God would be glorified in all that I wrote.

Thank you!

TABLE OF CONTENTS

PREFACE

"Evil is the most powerful word in the language and the most elusive." So claims *Time* essayist and author Lance Morrow. Remember the reaction Ronald Reagan got, Mr. Morrow asks, when he called Russia an "evil empire"? And remember the emotion George W. Bush evoked when he lumped several countries into an "axis of evil"? There is power in the word "evil."

Yet it is a hard word to pin down. Just think of all the questions that pop into your mind whenever the word "evil" is mentioned: How do you define it? Where did evil come from? Why does God allow it to mess up His beautiful world? Will evil ever be eradicated? These are questions most people think about at one time or another, I would imagine. And yes, the answers do seem to be elusive.

With the advent of suicide bombings, on-the-spot media coverage of natural disasters, and a statistical rise in the number of national and Christian leaders who have

XII · MAKING SENSE OF EVIL

fallen into sin, evil has become a hot topic. People want answers. Not just any answers. They want answers that make sense.

Enter Christian author Alister McGrath. "God gave us this world," he said in an interview in *World* magazine, (August 21, 2004), "and only God can make sense of it." But where does one go to get God's perspective on evil? you ask. To the place Christians have been going for centuries, I believe: the Bible. It is the only book where you will find such complex issues dealt with in depth and with accuracy you can trust.

Between Genesis and Revelation there are almost 600 references to evil. You will find the word associated with people, deeds, desires, and spirits (among an assortment of other things). God's choice of this particular word lends gravity to what might otherwise be described as simply "bad," "tragic," or "wrong."

As we go to the Bible, though, it helps to remember that the Scriptures do not reveal everything we may want to know. There are *"secret things"* that God keeps to Himself (Deuteronomy 29:29). So in a study as weighty as this one, we have to be prepared to leave some of our questions unanswered. We have to settle for the fact that when the finite tries to understand the infinite, there is only so far the finite can go.

The good news is that there are many things God *has* revealed. Those revealed things we are expected to master. So with this admonition in mind, let us begin trying to make sense of evil God's way, praying as we go that the Lord will open our eyes that we may see *"wonderful things"* in His law (Psalm 119:18).

Part One

Points to Ponder: A Study of Evil

"[T]hey…searched the scriptures daily [to see] whether those things were so."

—Acts 17:11 KJV

Chapter 1

EVIL REIGNS—OR DOES IT?

"The LORD has established his throne in heaven, and his kingdom rules over all."

—Psalm 103:19

The date was September 11, 2001; the time, 8:46 A.M. My husband Lee and I were listening to the radio as we went about our morning routine. Suddenly an emergency news bulletin grabbed our attention: "A plane has just hit the North Tower of the World Trade Center! We'll bring you more details as we get them."

This is not the first time a small aircraft had struck a New York City skyscraper, so our initial reaction was to minimize the severity of the crash. We did want to check out the scene, however, so each of us reached for a set of binoculars. (We live on the top floor of a high rise condominium on the Jersey shore, south of Manhattan.) We pointed our respective glasses northward and fine-tuned our lenses.

There they were, the two towering skyscrapers. But where was the plane? There was no sign of one, small or otherwise. Instead, we saw billows of smoke forcing their way out of the North Tower, and flames licking the building's frame. This was not the inconsequential accident we had expected to see. We turned on the TV for a closer look.

HIT AGAIN AND AGAIN

We watched the screen as fire engines and police cars rushed to the scene. Then the unthinkable happened: another plane slammed into the Trade Center, this time hitting the South Tower. Glued to the picture, we, like millions of others that day, became unwitting spectators to some very chilling scenes. We watched the fires as they spread. We gasped as office workers waved frantically from windows located above the flames, signaling their distress and growing hopelessness. Every once in a while we glimpsed a human figure plunging to the ground. The sight sickened us. Being burned alive or leaping to one's death—what a choice to have to make!

While these struggles were being shown on TV, others were taking place behind the scenes, we were told. Office workers were scrambling down smoke-filled stairways in a desperate attempt to reach safety. Most would make it. Others, sadly, would not.

A verbal trailer began to cross the screen: "At 9:38 A.M. American flight 77 plowed into the Pentagon in Washington, D.C.!" While we were trying to digest this new information, there was yet another blow: The South

Tower of the Trade Center, the second tower to be hit, was beginning to pancake. We held our breath as we watched it collapse. In four short seconds, those still trapped inside were turned to dust—simply pulverized!

MORE?

We found ourselves hoping the carnage was over. Reality, however, proved otherwise. Shortly after ten o'clock we learned that United flight 93 had crashed into a field in central Pennsylvania. This is the flight that, after being hijacked by terrorists, was turned toward a target in our nation's capital. Quick-thinking passengers banded together, reports later revealed. Motivated by the now-famous cry, "Let's roll!" these passengers moved en masse to overtake the hijackers. What happened after that no one knows for certain. But at a makeshift memorial erected near the crater that the doomed plane dug in the earth—a site Lee and I would later visit—a local spokesperson declared, "You folks are standing near the spot where America's first battle in the war against terrorism was fought and won." Not a single tourist present that day, including Lee and me, questioned the statement. Instead, we all remained speechless, lost in a silence that seemed almost sacred.

The reason Lee and I chose to visit the site of the crash of Flight 93 is that two of our church members, Don and Jean Peterson, were passengers on it. As their personal story unfolded, some disturbing facts emerged. It seems that Don and Jean had arrived for their 9:00 A.M. flight from Newark to San Francisco on September 11 with plenty of time to spare. While checking in, they were told they could switch to the 8:00 o'clock flight if they wished. They decided to make the change.

Family members, however, were not aware of this change. When the Petersons' son heard about the crash of a United flight to San Francisco leaving Newark at eight o'clock, he was concerned, we were told; yet at the same time, he was relieved. "Mom and Dad are on the nine o'clock," he reassured himself. "The eight o'clock is the one that went down. Phew!" It was not until later in the day that this son and other family members learned the awful truth about their loved ones' fatal decision.

MUSINGS

Let me say at this point that when a tragedy like 9/11 occurs, your mind can drive you crazy. *What ifs* and *if onlys* can haunt you. The Petersons' son probably thought, *What if Mom and Dad had not been so bent on getting to the airport early? If only they had stuck to their original schedule. Why did they decide to change flights?*

The Bible comes to our aid at times like these, reassuring us that there are no *what ifs* or *if onlys* with God. Whatever happens is part of an ultimate plan. While some people find such a conclusion disturbing, I find it wonderfully liberating. In fact, it is the only thing that sets one free from the bondage of the destructive *what-could-have-beens*.

As far as the Petersons are concerned, they had an appointment to meet their Maker on September 11, 2001. They kept that appointment. For them, death was not some cruel twist of fate. Rather, it was a planned homecoming. They got to experience its heartaches and joys together. They left Earth hand-in-hand.

This is not to say that Christian victims of tragedy escape the emotional and physical trauma that normally accompanies dreadful events. Nor does it mean that the Christians left behind do not experience the gut-wrenching sense of loss that all mourners feel. On the contrary, horror, pain, and emptiness can be the lot for Christians as well as for non-Christians, sometimes to a degree that is off the charts.

But let us not rule out God's power to intervene on behalf of His own. When Christ, in His high priestly prayer, asked the Father to *"protect"* His disciples *"from the evil one"* (John 17:15), He was not requesting an escape from suffering. He knew many of His followers would suffer deaths that would test their faith to the utmost. Rather, He was relying on what His Father would do in the midst of suffering. The Father would provide invisible *"shields"* to safeguard the soul, He knew (See Psalm 28:7), and send a *"peace"* that transcends human understanding to calm the troubled heart (See Philippians 4:7).

OPPORTUNITIES FOR A WITNESS

We were jolted out of our musings that day by a ringing phone. Lee answered it. The caller identified himself as Stephen Wilde, a radio host in Queenstown, New Zealand. While visiting the United States, Stephen had spent a week with us and knew that we had an unencumbered view of the World Trade Center in New York City. So when his station manager asked him to get someone from the greater New York City area on the line for an interview, Stephen knew just whom to call. Would Lee be willing to share what he was feeling? Of course. The question was, would Lee be able to?

In a voice quivering with emotion and with sirens wailing in the background (our local hospital was preparing to receive some of the injured), Lee bared his heart and his soul. The station manager later praised Stephen for his quick thinking and excellent interview. We were praising God that Lee was able to do the interview at all!

Later on, a friend, Rich Immordino, shared with us a unique opportunity he had to testify to his faith that day. It seems that Rich's office was located in a building near the Twin Towers. When the North Tower was hit, fellow workers crowded around his desk. Together they watched as the ensuing fire exploded into an inferno. And together they commiserated with those who were hanging out of windows crying for help. Everyone felt powerless. Suddenly into their view sped the second airliner. The group looked on in disbelief as the plane took aim at the South Tower and hit its target right on. There was a collective, audible gasp, Rich said. Then one fellow worker, who knew of Rich's Christian faith, caught Rich's eye and asked sarcastically, "OK, Mr. Immordino, where is your God now?"

"My God is in the same place today that He was in the day His Son died on Calvary's cross," Rich answered assuredly. "He's on His throne in heaven."

WORDS YOU CAN TRUST

There is a magnet on my refrigerator that reads, "Either God is in control or He isn't." To me that plaque says it all. You see, although events may *appear* to be spiraling out of control, that does not mean that they *are*. Although evil may *seem* to have gained the upper hand, that does not mean that it *has*. We live on a fallen planet. Ever since man sinned in the Garden of Eden, evil has been part of the curse God pronounced on humanity as a result of that sin. The curse *will* be with us until the end of time. But only until then. Jesus Christ will one day banish evil from the earth.

Meanwhile, God has Satan and his cohorts on a tether. They can go only so far. Unfortunately, these evildoers go as far as they can, and they do so every time. They strain at the very limits of God's unwelcome control. One day, however, they will be stopped in their tracks and duly punished for the harm they have done to God's people (See Isaiah 13:11). It will be a glorious day—a day of righteousness, justice, and truth.

We are talking about God's sovereignty. He has authority, power, rule, and control over everything that happens in His world. As philosopher Abraham Kuyper said, "There is not a square inch of the universe over which King Jesus does not claim, 'Mine.'"[1]

When the authors of the Bible address God's sovereignty, they do so with one voice and without equivocation. *"The Lord has established His throne in heaven,"* the psalmist asserts, *"and his kingdom rules over all"* (Psalm 103:19). God *"works out everything in conformity with the purpose of his will,"* the apostle Paul confirms (Ephesians 1:11). *"The kingdom of this world has become the kingdom of our Lord and of his Christ, and he will reign for ever and ever,"* the apostle John assures us as he glimpses the glories of heaven (Revelation 11:15). Christians, we either believe these words, or we do not. You see, when it comes to the sovereignty of God, there is no middle ground. As the plaque on my refrigerator says, "Either God is in control or He isn't."

Some Redeeming Features Of Tragedies

It is not unusual to hear Christians who have survived brutal manifestations of man's inhumanity to man testify that when things were darkest in their lives, they experienced God's redemptive power in ways they never could have imagined. "God went with me through *the valley of the shadow of death,"* some say; and I *"feared no evil"* (Psalm 23:4).

Others talk about the fact that things could have been worse. As far as the collapse of the Twin Towers is concerned, 15,000 people did manage to get out alive. While this statistic does little to relieve the pain of the families of the 2807 individuals who were crushed, it does show that there was a divine restraint on evil that day. It makes one wonder what the day would have been like without God's restraining hand.

Tragedies also serve as reminders that our days are numbered. They offer opportunities to get our souls right with God (See Psalm 90:12). According to reports from churches in our area, several people did put their trust in the Lord Jesus Christ as a result of 9/11. Others, sadly, did not. In fact, many are still ignoring the warning to repent of their sins and let God change their lives. How many more opportunities will they be granted? We do not know. What we do know is that one of these days Jesus Christ is going to revisit our planet and hold all His created beings accountable for their actions, both good and evil.

This can be a frightening thought. For when Jesus Christ comes again, He will not come as the sacrificial Lamb who *"takes away the sin of the world"* (John 1:29). Rather, this time He will come as the Lion of Judah, exacting judgment that is righteous and deserved (Revelation 5:5). At the time of His return, there will be no further opportunity to come to Him in repentance and faith. While this is bad news for those who do not know Him, it is wonderful news for those of us who do. For us, the return of Christ means an end to pain, sorrow, conflict, and death. It also means an end to evil. Yes, evil's days on earth are numbered.

IN SUMMARY

So what is the bottom line? Does evil reign on planet Earth? Absolutely not! The sovereign Lord reigns on planet Earth. This is *His* world, created by *His grace*, existing for *His* purposes.

Are we to ignore the evil we see around us then? No. For even though Christ won the battle against evil on the cross, Satan is a real and present danger. He fights on.

In the end, however, we know who comes out on top. It is the Lord. I invite you to visit the former site of the World Trade Center and look for two large steel girders welded together. Forming a cross, they stand alone in the emptiness of the towers' footprints. This "cross" was discovered by the cleanup crew, reverently set aside, and then positioned on the crash site as a symbol of hope. For the Christian, however, this "cross" symbolizes more than hope. It symbolizes victory, now and forever.

It is thrilling to realize that at this very moment, the sovereign Lord, from His throne on high, is fitting everything that happens on our planet into a plan that was conceived even before the world was created. One day we Christians will be privileged to view the blueprint of that plan, I imagine, and we will marvel at how the darker pieces of the puzzle were designed to fit into the lighter ones. Right now, however, we are plagued by questions. We know we are on the winning side, but we cannot help yearning for the end of evil's destruction. When will it come?

Interestingly, the Bible tells us more about evil's end than it does about its beginning, but that does not stop us from wondering. Where did evil come from? How did it get started? Did its presence catch God off guard? I invite you to join me as together we dig for some answers to these very provocative questions.

Chapter 2

Evil Emerged in Eden— or Was It Earlier?

"'You will not surely die,' the serpent said to the woman. 'For God knows that when you eat of [the forbidden fruit], your eyes will be opened, and you will be like God, knowing good and evil.'"

—Genesis 3:4,5

G od had just completed His work of creation. Everything He had made was good. In fact, He pronounced it *"very good,"* the Bible says (Genesis 1:31). There was no evil in Eden.

One day, however, all that changed. In response to the tempting of a *"serpent"* (Genesis 3:1), Eve reached for fruit from *"the tree of the knowledge of good and evil,"* the only tree God had declared off limits, and ate it. Then she offered some fruit to her husband Adam, who, the Bible says, was *"with her"* (Genesis 3:6). He too ate it. And that is how sin entered God's perfect world.

With sin's entrance came changes. The first man and first woman noticed they were naked, so they sewed fig leaves together in an attempt to cover themselves (Genesis 3:7). God, however, saw right through their self-made coverings, right to the sinful condition of their hearts. They were in need of *His* covering—a covering He symbolically provided in the skins of slain animals (see Genesis 3:21).

Another change that Adam and Eve experienced was a loss of closeness to their Creator. When the Lord invited them to walk with Him in the cool of the day (as they had been accustomed to doing up to then), they ran and hid (Genesis 3:8). They seemed to sense they were no longer worthy of fellowship with a God who is holy. This rift would one day be bridged by the cross. Right then, however, in the Garden of Eden, sin was making its consequences known.

A third change the first couple noticed was how easy it now was to lie. Whereas truth used to spring naturally from their lips, both now found it convenient to avoid answers that were direct. They also shifted blame for their actions (see Genesis 3:12,13). It is not a huge stretch to assume that these equivocations disrupted the harmony of their marriage.

As more and more of sin's consequences pervaded Eden's paradise, the Lord made some pronouncements that showed how offended He is when people disobey His commands. The pronouncements He made then instill fear even today, yet at the same time they offer hope. Contemplate the bittersweet nature of what the Lord prophesied:

1. The evil *"serpent"* would one day be defeated, but
   not before he caused more trouble for God's people
   (Genesis 3:14,15).
2. A woman would eventually give birth to a Deliverer,
   but only through a process so painful every woman
   would come to dread it (Genesis 3:16).
3. Man would continue to be productive in his work,
   but only through *"sweat"* would he now see results
   (Genesis 3:19).
4. Marriage would continue to be a foretaste of the
   perfect union the redeemed would one day enjoy
   with the Bridegroom Christ (Revelation 19:7,8), but
   in the meantime, earthly union would be marred
   by the desire of each partner to dominate the other
   (Genesis 3:16).

How challenging these struggles would prove to be in
the days ahead.

Sadly, there was one more "curse" on fallen humanity.
It was this: Every person born from Adam's day forward
would have to deal with the devastating process of aging.
Men and women alike would be forced to watch their bodies
deteriorate. Yes, these "earthsuits" of ours are degenerating
a little bit each day. (I don't have to tell you this!) And they
will continue to do so until death claims them and they
return to the earth from which they came (Genesis 3:19).
Relegated to dust, these bodies will remain in the grave until
God calls them forth (John 5:28,29). But God *will* call them
forth. That is a promise. There *will* be a resurrection. This
is good news. In fact, we have good news in every one of
the Lord's predictions. We can not help being brought up

short by the bad news, however. And we can not help being overwhelmed by the myriad of problems that has gripped our entire world—all through a single act of disobedience! So, it appears evil began in the Garden of Eden. Or did it?

BACK UP A BIT

Meet Satan, a spiritual being who is generally portrayed as the personification of evil. The Bible describes him as the *"father of lies"* (John 8:44), an *"accuser of our brothers"* (Revelation 12:10), a *"roaring lion looking for someone to devour"* (1 Peter 5:8), one who is bent on leading *"the whole world astray"* (Revelation 12:9).

Yet Satan, it appears, started out good. Like all the angels (Satan is a fallen angel), he originally had access to the throne of God (Job 1:6). This was the place where celestial beings received instructions. It was also the place where they could express their delight in what their Creator was doing. When God spoke the earth into existence, the angels joined the stars in shouting for joy, the Bible says (Job 38:7). It was a time of celebration.

Participating in this happy chorus, presumably, was Satan, who, beneath his joyful exterior, nurtured a selfish ambition. *What a great place the earth would be to* foil *the plan of God!* he was probably thinking. *I wonder if I can tempt those humans to sin.*

So, it seems that evil was taking shape even before Adam and Eve tasted the fruit, does it not? No wonder Jesus called Satan *"a murderer from the beginning"* (John 8:44). He was. And he is still about his dastardly business.

What were the circumstances surrounding Satan's fall? There is not an obvious answer in the Bible. Rather, the answer is hidden in descriptions that have primary references to historical persons and circumstances and only secondary references to the evil one behind those historical persons and circumstances.

As we look at two of these veiled references, let us remember that hidden, deeper meanings are not unusual in the Bible. Throughout the Old Testament the person and work of the Lord Jesus Christ is prefigured in historical people. Moses delivered God's people from bondage and led them to the Promised Land. Aaron, the high priest, went into the presence of God, offering a blood sacrifice to atone for sin. So we ask, is the evil one's person and work spoken of in a veiled way as well? Many Bible scholars think so. They feel that several biblical references to evil have meaning well beyond the persons and situations of their day.

One of these references is from the book of Ezekiel. While addressing the King of Tyre, Satan's tool at that particular time in human history, the prophet hints at evil's origin in the Garden of Eden, personified in Satan:

> *"You were the model of perfection*
> *full of wisdom and perfect in beauty.*
> *You were in Eden, the Garden of God....*
> *You were anointed as a guardian cherub;*
> *for so I ordained you....*
> *You were blameless in all your ways*
> *from the day you were created*
> *till wickedness was found in you."*
>
> —Ezekiel 28:11–15

Let us pause here for a moment. The text says, *"till wickedness was found in you."* Does the author's use of the passive voice mean that evil just "appeared" one day in the subject's heart, that he had nothing to do with its entrance, that he was a victim, rather than a perpetrator of his crime?

Definitely not. We must keep on reading, for further along in the account, Ezekiel says of his subject, *"You sinned"* (v 16). This is a phrase the apostle Peter applies to *all* the angels that fell (see 2 Peter 2:4). And it is a concept the prophet Isaiah elaborates upon when he expresses the idea that sin—any sin—rarely just "happens." Rather, it is actively, willingly, and knowingly committed. To prove his point, Isaiah describes Babylon (and the evil figure, arguably Satan, who is behind the sins of Babylon) in the following way:

> *"How you have fallen from heaven,*
> *O morning star, son of the dawn!...*
> *You said in your heart,*
> *'I will ascend to heaven;*
> *I will raise my throne*
> *above the stars of God;*
> *I will sit enthroned on the mount*
> *of assembly,*
> *on the utmost heights of the sacred*
> *mountain.*
> *I will ascend to the tops of the clouds;*
> *I will make myself like the Most High'"*
>
> —Isaiah 14:12–14

With this string of *"I wills,"* we see a heart bent on rebellion—a heart filled with prideful ambition. It is this ambition that brought down the *"morning star,"* Isaiah says (14:12). The apostle John, in his vision on Patmos, referred to a *"star that had fallen from the sky to the earth"* (Revelation 9:1). And Jesus told his disciples He watched *"Satan fall like lightning from heaven"* (Luke 10:18). The three descriptions seem to be of the same being.

Satan paid dearly for his desire to rise above the position God assigned him, and so did his cohorts. According to the apostle John, this one who fought Michael and his band of good angels was *"hurled from heaven to the abode of the earth, along with his entire army"* (Revelation 12:9). The abode of God was no longer a place any of them could call home. An even worse punishment, however, awaits them. One day Satan and his angels will be relegated to a place of *"eternal fire,"* the Bible says (Matthew 25:41)—and all because of personal ambition that dared to challenge the authority of God.

The precise timing of Satan's downfall is a matter of debate among Bible scholars. What we do know, however, is that at some point it did occur. We also know that Satan is limited in how much evil he can accomplish. He cannot be everywhere at once, he does not know everything that is going to happen, and he is not more powerful than God. In fact, his plans are subject to the overall will of the One who created him.

BACK UP FARTHER

So, when did evil have its beginnings? Was it with the sin of Adam and Eve in the Garden? Was it before that, with

Satan's rebellion in pre-earth eternity? Or was it even before that, in the pre-creation counsels of the Godhead?

One thing we can say for sure: the entrance of evil was not a surprise to the Almighty. He did not suddenly have to switch to Plan B because Plan A got messed up by some force He could not control. No way! He is the sovereign Lord. He rules over all His creation. Nothing happens outside His perfect will (either outside His direct command or outside His working through secondary means). This belief in God's sovereign control is bedrock to the Christian faith. The Bible says, *"Who can speak and have it happen if the Lord has not decreed it? Is it not from the mouth of the Most High that both calamities and good things come?"* (Lamentations 3:37,38). So, when it comes to trying to explain how evil originated, we might summarize it this way: God decreed the existence of evil and was able to do so without becoming part of it.

In other words, from the beginning of time, evil was part of God's plan—not part of God's nature or character, mind you—that would be impossible and blasphemous to imply—but part of God's plan for His world. For without the advent of evil, there would be nothing with which to contrast good and, thus, no way to define good. There would also be no choice between sinning and not sinning. No sin, no Fall. No Fall, no need for a cross. And without the cross, God could not show the world His love, His mercy, and His grace.

"Evil is caused by human sin," says author Richard Gamble, "yet it is also part of God's sovereign plan."[2] The apostle Paul agrees. He says, *"For God has bound all men over to disobedience so that he may have mercy on them all"* (Romans 11:32). As Paul was making this statement, he must have been struck by its profound implications, for immediately he burst into praise. He exclaimed:

> *"O, the depth of the riches and the*
> *wisdom and knowledge of God!*
> *How unsearchable his judgments*
> *and his paths beyond tracing out!*
> *Who has known the mind of the Lord?*
> *Or who has been his counselor?*
> *Who has ever given to God*
> *that God should repay him?*
> *For from him and through him and to him*
> *are all things.*
> *To him be the glory forever! Amen."*
>
> —Romans 11:33–36

Do not these words make you want to burst into your own exclamation of praise? Paul is saying that God is the source of all things. God is the means through whom all things come. And God's glory is the end of everything that happens. What Bible-believing Christian can argue with that? What Bible-believing Christian would want to?

THINK ABOUT WHO GOD IS

God is holy. God is perfect. God is good. In Him there is *"no darkness at all,"* the Bible declares (1 John 1:5). In other words, the Lord, by His very nature, is distinct from

His creatures and separate from their sin. His character is free from impurity, even from the slightest taint or hint of wrongdoing. Therefore, it is *unthinkable* to conclude that evil sprang from His being.

However, God is also sovereign. He is in control of everything that happens in heaven and on earth (Psalm 103:19). So, while it is blasphemous to imply that evil sprang from God's holy nature, it is equally blasphemous to imply that God had no control over its appearance. To dispel any doubt about this matter, the Lord speaks to the origin of evil. *"And it is I,"* He asserts in the writing of Isaiah, *"who have created the destroyer to work havoc"* (Isaiah 54:16). He also says, *"I form light and create darkness; I make peace and create evil. I, the Lord, do all these things"* (Isaiah 45:6,7 KJV).

Fellow believers, do not be troubled by these assertions. They do not mean God is out to get you. Quite the contrary. What they mean is that from the beginning the sovereign Lord has been directing, and will continue to direct, all your difficulties to an end that is holy, righteous, and good. Therefore, you can trust Him with your life, now and always. Pastor Rick Warren in his best-selling book *The Purpose-Driven Life* agrees. He says, "Everything that happens to a child of God is Father-filtered, and he intends to use it for good even when Satan and others mean it for bad."[3]

Stop to think: Would you want it any other way? Would you not rather have a God in charge of evil than a God shocked by it? Does it not bring you comfort to know that your troubles are in hands that are capable of turning them into blessings, rather than in hands being wrung in despair? Are you not glad you do not have to wonder whether God will win the battle this time? Of course He will. He wins *every* time.

The amazing thing about all of this, however, is not God's decree to render the existence of evil certain or, once it exists, to use it for good. Rather, it is God's ability to make use of evil without "touching" it or without allowing it to "touch" Him. You see, God can direct evil to a holy end without becoming personally tainted by it. As I said before, evil can be part of God's plan without becoming part of His person.

But why would evil be part of a good God's plan? How can it serve Him? What is its ultimate purpose? More answers—and, yes, more questions—lie ahead.

Chapter 3

Evil Serves Satan—Does It Also Serve God?

"The Lord works out everything for his own ends—even the wicked for the day of disaster."

—Proverbs 16:4

Imagine you are present at the first performance of a newly completed symphony. You know the composer personally, so you are excited to be in the audience. On this night your friend is conducting his own work. As you listen to the music he has composed, you find yourself paying special attention to each and every nuance. You want to be able to give an informed response when you greet your friend at the end of the evening.

The work as a whole is quite impressive, you conclude. The composition reflects artistry, the harmony is pleasing to the ear, and the tempo seems just right. The listening experience is proving to be so pleasant, in fact, that you feel yourself sinking deeper and deeper into your seat. *How relaxing! How lyrical! How lovely!*

Suddenly you bolt upright in your chair. The music has shifted to a minor key. The brass is intruding with dissonant staccato sounds, and the violins are screeching discordantly. *Stop! Stop! Stop!* your mind screams as your hands fly up to cover your ears. *Saboteurs must have sneaked into this performance with the intent of disrupting it! No competent composer would write such confusion and discord!*

How wrong you are! Your composer friend *did* write what you are hearing. The orchestra is playing exactly what it has been given. This movement, with its minor key and lack of harmony, has been included for a purpose. But what is that purpose? As you attempt to answer this question, you....

THINK ABOUT LIFE

"Life is a symphony," writes Christian composer Beatrice Bush Bixler.[4] Unfortunately, not all of it is lived in close harmony. There are periods of discord and dissonance. This discord may come in the form of a terrorist attack, as it did on 9/11/2001; or it may come as a devastating tsunami, as it did on 12/26/2004. It may come as a hurricane named Katrina or Rita; or it may come more personally, as when a loved one is snatched by death, when a debilitating illness strikes, or when a precious relationship is hopelessly broken. Whatever form discord takes, it impacts a lot of things: what we think about, what we talk about, and how we act.

In times of distress, life shifts to a minor key. Despair hangs in the air. There are disappointments where there used to be hope, heartaches where there once was joy, and plans on how to survive instead of decisions on what exciting thing to do next. In times like these, where do we turn for help?

We turn to God if we are wise. The Composer of life's symphony is poised to come to our rescue. *"Don't let your heart be troubled,"* Jesus Christ tells us. *"Trust in God; trust also in me"* (John 14:1). *"I am removing 'what can be shaken—that is, created things—so that what cannot be shaken may remain'"* (Hebrews 12:27). Friends, the kingdom of our Lord is one of those things that *"cannot be shaken"* (v 28). So let us praise His holy name for a spiritual foundation that remains strong, even when everything else is being swept away.

BLESSED ASSURANCE

When things go wrong in our individual spheres of influence, Scripture gives us several reasons to hang in there. The first is this: life's symphony will end well for those who have committed their lives to the Lord Jesus Christ. The trials we face in this present life will be worked for our spiritual good, the Bible says (See Romans 8:28–30). Life's distressing minor key will one day modulate to a major one, *"achieving for us an eternal glory that far outweighs them all"* (2 Corinthians 4:17). But this is true only for those who are trusting Christ to work things out. For those who are trying to work things out on their own, there is no promise from God to resolve the discord in their lives.

Second, present pain, in light of eternity, is really quite short-lived. As trying as a current situation may be, it will last only for a moment in the larger scheme of things, the Bible says (see Romans 8:18). This is good news. When we know an unpleasant experience has an end, we have motivation to persevere. This realization is probably one of many factors that encouraged our Savior as He was dying for our sins. *"[F]or the joy set before him, [He] endured the cross, scorning its shame, and sat down at the right hand of the throne of God"*, the Bible says. Then it continues: *"Consider him who endured such opposition from sinful men, so that you will not grow weary and lose heart"* (Hebrews 12:2,3). In these verses God's Word is pointing us to the perfect role model, Jesus Christ, for encouragement to persevere in time of trouble.

Third, the Lord is in control of the whole "musical score," both of the lyrical movements of life and of the heavier ones as well. *"I know the plans I have for you,"* declares the Lord, *"plans to prosper you and not to harm you, plans to give you hope and a future"* (Jeremiah 29:11). This promise was given to God's people, the Israelites, in one of their darkest hours. Exiled to Babylon because of their many transgressions, the Israelites were far from their beloved homeland and their familiar worship rituals. Venting their frustrations, they hung their harps on poplar trees by the Kebar River and let their sorrow spill out (See Ezekiel 1:1 and Psalm 137:1–3). They could see no escape from the evildoers who were presently holding them captive.

But there would be an escape. God was working it out even at the moment of their deepest depression. He would soften the hearts of Israel's oppressors to the point that not only would they return the Israelites to their homeland, but they would facilitate the rebuilding of their Holy City and of their temple as well. Life's temporary discord would turn to harmony again—and it would all be orchestrated by the One whose plan includes life's every detail, the dark as well as the light, the heavy as well as the lyrical, the mournful as well as the joyful.

Greek author Sophocles once said, "One must wait until the evening to see how bright the day has been." How true! Think about it. Does not darkness cause an appreciation for light? Winter for spring? Illness for health? Work for play? Hatred for love? War for peace? Law for grace? And does not the presence of evil evoke a yearning for the triumph of good? Of course. That is how the symphony of life has been scripted. The Bible puts it this way: *"As long as the earth endures, seedtime and harvest, cold and heat, summer and winter, day and night will never cease"* (Genesis 8:22). We need all these things. One part of the coupling has no meaning without the other. Composers of symphonies understand this. So does the Composer of life's musical score.

WORDS OF CAUTION

The fact that evil is part of God's plan for the Earth, however, does not mean that God approves of it. On the contrary, He *"hates"* it, the Bible says (see Hebrews 1:9). Furthermore, the Bible makes clear that He *"hates"* all who commit it as well (see Psalm 5:5,6). How can this be? you ask. It cannot be otherwise. For without evildoers, moral evil remains a remote concept. With evildoers it becomes a reality. Evildoers are the ones who choose to engage in what a holy God abhors. In other words, without people to commit it, there is no such thing as wrongdoing.

Second, the fact that God uses evil to accomplish purposes that are holy does not mean He excuses sin. On the contrary, God will hold sinners accountable for each and every wrongdoing they perpetrate. *"I will punish the world for its evil,"* He says, *"the wicked for their sins"* (Isaiah 13:11). A day of reckoning is coming. Nobody gets away with sinning for long. Evildoers will be judged because what they have done is an offense to everything God is: holiness, righteousness, and goodness.

Third, the fact that God uses the ungodly, as well as the godly, to carry out His purposes does not mean people are puppets in His hand. Rather, they are free agents—agents who act without coercion or manipulation. Ask them. They will tell you they are doing what they desire to do. The fact that a sovereign Lord might be superintending their actions and fitting them into a plan that is ultimately redemptive is the farthest thing from their minds. As far as they are concerned, they are simply exercising their rights as humans (or demons) to make their own decisions and to execute those decisions any way they please. They are acting of their own free will, according to their own sinful natures.

In the final analysis, however, everything, evil acts included, must submit to the purposes of the sovereign Lord. Evil can go only so far. At some point its influence will be stopped altogether. But until that moment, God reserves the right to use it. And what He uses it for is good. Why do we humans have so much trouble accepting the fact that evil is a tool in God's hands? Authors Bayne and Hinlicky make an observation. "It is easier to accept a world spun out of control, with evil abounding," they say, "than a world ordered by God where evil has a chosen place."[5]

GRACE NOTES

I am humbled when I think of how God used the greatest evil the world has ever known to accomplish the greatest good. It occurred on Mount Calvary outside Jerusalem two thousand years ago, when the Son of God was crucified for sins He did not commit. He was nailed to a cross by *"wicked"* men, the Bible tells us, yet these *"wicked"* men accomplished *"God's set purpose,"* (Acts 2:23). Through His death and resurrection, Jesus Christ disarmed these powers bent on His destruction and made *"a public spectacle of them,"* we are told (Colossians 2:15).

Not only was God victorious over evil, He was not surprised when it showed its ugly face in the events leading up to the cross. Think about it. When the Sanhedrin set out to silence a rabble rouser named Jesus, did the Father bring His hand to His mouth in shock? Or when one of Jesus' disciples betrayed Him in the Garden of Gethsemane, did the Son of God scratch His head and cry, "What do I do now?" Or when the mob began screaming *"Crucify! Crucify!"* did the Father feel as if His beautiful "musical score" were being hijacked by saboteurs and rewritten by the powers of evil?

Of course not. His symphony was being played exactly as it had been scripted, down to the *"thirty pieces of silver"* Judas would be paid to deliver Jesus to the self-righteous religious authorities of the day (see Zechariah 11:13).

What is most surprising about the evil events surrounding the cross, however, is not that they happened exactly as planned, it is that they were motivated by God's love, mercy, and grace. Who would guess, for example, that mankind would discover God's love because God's Son endured His Father's wrath? Or who would think that for sinners to receive God's mercy, Jesus Christ would have to experience God's judgment? Or who could imagine that in order for the religious to be saved from their sin, their promised Redeemer would have to be struck down? No one. Yet that is exactly how divine love, mercy, and grace manifested themselves to men and women on earth: through an evil act, committed by evil men, and used by God to redeem lost sinners.

SO WHAT'S THE VERDICT?

Is evil a problem to God? Not really. We are talking about the Great I Am, the Creator of everything that is, the Alpha and Omega, the First Cause behind all secondary causes, the One who has ordained "whatsoever comes to pass"[6] and has done so not only for His own name's sake but also for the benefit of all who trust in Him.

As we are extolling the virtues of our sovereign Lord, however, it behooves us not to confuse the way *He* works with the way *we* work. For example, He is proactive; we are reactive. We respond to what happens and change our plans accordingly. God does not. He may change a human circumstance in response to prayer, but His eternal decrees remain steadfast.

Second, we humans become defensive when attacked by the enemy. God is on the offensive all the time. He can wipe out His blasphemers in an instant if He wants to. Instead, He lets them experience His longsuffering. He is in total control of the "game" of life.

Third, we humans mess up time and time again. God never messes up. Everything He does He does well. Furthermore, He does it well the first time around. There are no erasure marks on the score of His symphony. What the orchestra members play is what the Composer originally wrote. This they do freely, using the talents they have been given. It all leads up to one grand finale. When that finale comes, life as we know it will be no more. *"The heavens will disappear with a roar,"* the Bible says; *"the elements will be destroyed by fire, and the earth and everything in it will be laid bare"* (2 Peter 3:10). Dissonance! Discord! Minor keys!

But Then...

In the midst of all the trouble and chaos, the sovereign Lord will make a grand appearance. When He does, He will create *"a new heavens and a new earth,"* the Bible says (Revelation 21:11). Chaos will give way to tranquility, and sin to perfect righteousness. Satan and his cohorts will be thrown into the *"lake of burning sulphur,"* never to harass God's people again (Revelation 20:10). And God's redeemed will gather round His throne in praise, singing hallelujah to the Lamb. *"Salvation and glory and power belong to our God,"* the chorus will exclaim, *"for true and just are his judgments. He has condemned the great prostitute who corrupted the earth by her adulteries. He has avenged on her the blood of his servants"* (Revelation 19:2).

At this point the orchestra will modulate into a major key, I imagine. Then for a split second it will stop playing altogether. There will be a moment of sacred silence. The audience will hold its breath. Then, in a burst of hair-raising, spine-tingling glory, trumpets will sound, drums will roll, cymbals will clash, and the heavenly choir will chime in with one last harmonious chord. That chord will be God's triumphant "Amen" to life's grand and glorious symphony.

With the sound of the finale still echoing throughout the chambers of heaven, I envision the audience rising to its feet in thunderous applause. The Composer/Conductor places His baton on the music stand, faces the audience, takes His customary bow, and signals the orchestra members to stand with Him. All the while, the applause is continuing. And continuing. And continuing. "Bravo, Maestro, bravo!" rises above the din. It is the cry of God's "redeemed." It is a grateful cry. An exuberant cry. A cry that will keep on ringing throughout eternity.

Yes, the Lord is in the business of making something beautiful out of things gone horribly wrong. That is what the word "redeemed" means. As a result, multitudes of sinners will receive hope in a future that is glorious.

As we think about the redemption of "sinners," however, a question naturally arises: Do all people fall into the "sinners" category? Or is there a special group of people who are really evil—"bad seeds" from the start? More mind-stretching thoughts are coming. Stay with us.

Chapter 4

EVIL TURNS GOOD PEOPLE BAD—OR ARE ALL BAD FROM THE START?

"No one is good—except God alone."

—Mark 10:18

D
o you remember how you felt right after you became a parent for the first time? Watching new life come into the world is a spiritual experience of the highest order! But the greatest blessing comes when you take your brand new baby into your arms.

As you gaze down upon the little face framed in a soft yellow blanket, you are intent on scrutinizing every tiny detail. How precious are the sleeping eyes, sealed by long, dark lashes. How slight the mound that is the baby's nose. You place a finger beneath the tiny nostrils and keep it there long enough to feel puffs of air escaping in rhythm. Gently, you touch the rosy cheeks and caress the tiny lips—lips that seem to suggest a smile. *What a picture of tranquility this little bundle is!* you think. *May this moment last forever!*

It is not to be. In no time at all the blanketed form cradled in your elbow begins to stir. *Uh oh!* The relaxed eyelids pop open in alarm. The bound arms work their way free. The tiny feet, still covered, begin to kick. Then you watch as those perfectly formed little lips part widely, revealing a cavernous gap. Suddenly, out of the depths emerges a wail that would put the local fire siren to shame. The howl goes on and on. The only relief you get is when those tiny lungs run out of air. Then for a second there is silence—until the lungs fill again, that is. Then out comes another blast—one that is even more piercing than the first. *Somebody come and take this baby! Quick!*

As you are waiting for relief, you study your charge. The brow is furrowed now, the eyes have narrowed into slits, the hands have tightened into fists, and the cheeks are red with rage. What a horrible change has taken place in your tiny, peaceful bundle! You can hardly believe the difference. Unfortunately, this metamorphosis is a harbinger of things to come.

Over the next few months, you experience more unnerving episodes; and not all, you discover, are related to hunger, wetness, or pain. Some are simply old-fashioned temper tantrums; and they cause embarrassment beyond measure, especially when they occur in public. You begin to wonder what in the world you have produced.

One day you remember an article you cut out of the local paper a long time ago. It was a report given by the Minnesota Crime Commission in an attempt to explain heightened crime statistics. Although the Commission was a secular one, the conclusions the group came to were surprisingly biblical. Perhaps that is why you saved the article all these

years. Curious, you read it again. This time th.
even more significance:

> *Every baby starts life as a little savage. He is comple*
> *selfish and self-centered. He wants what he wants when ,*
> *wants it—his bottle, his mother's attention, his playmate's*
> *toy, his uncle's watch. Deny these and he seethes with rage*
> *and aggressiveness which would be murderous were he not*
> *so helpless. He is, in fact, dirty. He has no morals, no knowl-*
> *edge, no skills. This means that all children, not just certain*
> *children, are born delinquent. If permitted to continue in the*
> *self-centered world of his infancy, given free reign to his*
> *impulsive actions, to satisfy his wants, every child would*
> *grow up a criminal, a thief, a killer, and a rapist....*

Glory be! you think to yourself. *The Commission has just
described my baby! Is their assessment accurate? Are their
words true? Is human nature really this depraved?*

WHAT DOES GOD SAY?

The Bible agrees with the commission's assessment.
Human nature is in sad shape, riddled through and through
with sin. *"For from within, out of men's hearts,"* Jesus explained
to his followers, *"come evil thoughts, sexual immorality,
theft, murder, adultery, greed, malice, deceit, lewdness, envy,
slander, arrogance, and folly"* (Matthew 15:19). *"There is
no one righteous, not even one,"* the apostle Paul tells the
Romans (Romans 3:10); *"there is no one who does good"*
(v 12); *"for all have sinned and fall short of the glory of God"*
(v 23). To claim otherwise is to bury one's head in the sand.

Or as the apostle John so aptly puts it, *"If we claim to be without sin, we deceive ourselves"* (1 John 1:18).

Sin, the Bible teaches, touches every aspect of our being—from the top of our heads to the tip of our toes. Consider the heart, the wellspring of life. *"The heart is deceitful above all things,"* the prophet Jeremiah declares, *"and beyond cure"* (17:9). Consider the mind. *"The unregenerate are darkened in their understanding,"* the apostle Paul adds, *"and separated from the life of God because of the ignorance that is in them due to the hardening of their hearts"* (Ephesians 4:18). Consider what the other body parts are like before Christ comes in. *"Their throats are open graves,"* the apostle Paul continues, *"their tongues practice deceit. The poison of vipers is on their lips. Their mouths are full of cursing and bitterness. Their feet are swift to shed blood....There is no fear of God before their eyes"* (Romans 3:13–18). It sounds as if we members of the human race need total body makeovers, does it not? In fact, we do.

But are we as bad as we could be? Thankfully, no. Why not? Because the sovereign Lord restrains evil. As a result, only a few human beings are permitted to give themselves over to evil's full reign. These few—we are talking now about people like Nero, Caligula, Hitler, Stalin, Mao Tse Tung, Pol Pot, Idi Amin, Saddam Hussein, Osama bin Ladin and more—cause pain beyond measure and do so to countless numbers of law-abiding citizens. Yet over the course of human history, thankfully the number of those who are victimized far exceeds the number of those who inflict harm.

The most frightening aspect of a study like this, however, is not what these recognized monsters did and what people like them will continue to do; it is what we ourselves are capable of doing if presented with the right set of circumstances. It is reported that when the Nazi Adolf Eichmann was put on trial for his crimes against the Jews, CBS's Mike Wallace interviewed a Holocaust survivor who testified at the Nuremburg trial. The survivor collapsed on the floor in tears when he saw Eichmann, Wallace reported.

Later Wallace asked the survivor if he had reacted as he did because he saw evil in the eyes of a monster. The survivor replied, "No, it was because I saw the capacity in myself to do the same thing."[7] Yes, the potential for evil lies within each of us. The most innocent of babies can turn into a brutal savage if given the right set of circumstances.

Think about yourself. How good are you at practicing self-control? How, for example, might you react if someone slandered your good name and you could not prove yourself innocent? How would you handle yourself if a trusted friend swindled you out of your life's savings, even lured you into friendship with such a crime in mind? What might you do if your daughter were raped by a sex offender whom you had, in ignorance, hired to do odd jobs around the house? Be glad God restrains people's natural tendencies, your own included. If He did not, our world would be in even worse shape than it is; for some incredibly terrible things can happen when the human tendency to sin is allowed to run amok. It makes us wonder, though, how the capacity for evil we see in ourselves came to be part of us.

BACK TO THE GARDEN

As we saw earlier, the Bible attributes the human capacity for evil to what Bible scholars call "the Fall." Colonial children of the United States were taught the significance of this event when learning their ABCs. "A is for Adam," the New England Primer instructed them; "In Adam's fall we sinned all." This rhyme was a catchy way of introducing the theological truth that has become known as "original sin." Original sin is passed down from Adam to succeeding generations. There is no escaping it. "Intellectually we may balk at the doctrine of original sin," says author William Edgar, "but descriptively, as Blaine Pascal suggested, it is the best thing going, because it accounts for what we observe and feel."[8]

The patriarch Job agrees. *"Who can bring what is pure from the impure?"* he asks, voicing his own frustration. Then he answers, *"No one"* (Job 14:4). The apostle Paul, in his letter to the Romans, says, *"the result of one trespass* (Adam's sin) *was condemnation for all men"* (Romans 5:18). Then he emphasizes, *"through the disobedience of one man* (Adam) *the many were made sinners"* (v 19).

King David, you will remember, recognized his inherited sin nature as one source of his problem with lust. After committing adultery with Bathsheba and having her husband murdered as part of the cover-up, he exclaimed, *"Surely I was sinful at birth, sinful from the time my mother conceived me"* (Psalm- 51:5). He would have agreed with the way some wise theologians express sinful tendencies today. "We are not sinners because we sin," they say; "we sin because we are sinners."

Adam's sin has been passed on to his descendants in at least two ways. First of all, as humanity's "father," Adam has contributed his progeny's "genes," not only their physical genes but also their "spiritual genes." In other words, he has given his offspring their sin natures. Second, in sinning, Adam became humanity's representative or "federal head." When he ate the forbidden fruit, he was acting on behalf of his constituency down through the ages. That constituency includes every human being who has ever lived, is living now, or will live hereafter.

The Verdict?

We are all guilty! And not just because we are born with a sin nature. We are all guilty because we all choose to sin as well. You see, sin is more than a state of being. It is also a personal choice, a conscious decision of the will. After the Bible tells us that *"sin entered the world by one man and death through sin,"* it adds, *"and in this way death came to all men because all have sinned"* (Romans 5:12). Both aspects of sin (the state of being and the personal choice) are presented here in the same sentence. Why? Because they go together. Everyone who has a sin nature sins. Everybody who sins has a sin nature.

In the book of Ephesians, the apostle Paul talks of people being *"darkened in their understanding"* (Note the passive voice). But then the verb changes to the active voice. *"Having lost all sensitivity,* [the unregenerate] *have given themselves over to sensuality so as to indulge in every kind of impurity, with a continual lust for more,"* the author says (Ephesians 4:19). This *"indulging"* and *"lusting,"* describes everybody. *"All of us also lived among* [the unregenerate] *at one time"*, the apostle makes clear, *"gratifying the cravings of our sinful nature and following its desires and thoughts"* (Ephesians 2:3). In other words, we humans may be born slaves of sin, but we also choose to do it. *All* of us choose to sin! You and I, too!

Even when we choose *not* to do something, we can be sinning. For example, if we are made aware of a need in someone's life and it is within our ability to meet that need, yet we do nothing at all about it, we are guilty of deliberately ignoring the Spirit's nudgings. Listen to the words of the apostle James: *"Anyone who knows the good he ought to do and doesn't do it, sins"* (James 4:17). This sounds like a Catch-22, does it not?

But the worst is yet to come. For the Bible says that even Christians—those of us who, in Christ, have been given new natures—natures that *can* choose to do good in the eyes of God—find ourselves struggling with sin. Consider what the apostle Paul says about himself. *"When I want to do good,"* he laments, *"evil is right there with me. For in my inner being, I delight in God's law; but I see another law at work in the members of my body, waging war against the law of my mind and making me a prisoner of the law of sin at work within my members. What a wretched man that I am! Who will rescue me from this body of death? Thanks be to God—through Jesus Christ our Lord!"* (Romans 7:21–25).

FREE AT LAST!

Yes, there is victory in Jesus. On Calvary's cross God's Son paid the penalty for the sins of all who would believe in Him. How did He do it? By taking those sins upon Himself. The Father *"made Him who knew no sin,"* the Bible says, *"to be sin for us so that in Him we might become the righteousness of God"* (2 Corinthians 5:21).

When Christ died, He dealt with *all* aspects of sin: the guilt, the curse, and the punishment. Because Christ took sin's guilt, we who trust in Him can have consciences that are clear; we can sleep at night. Because Christ took sin's curse, we who are born in Adam's line can live curse-free; we have been released from spiritual bondage. And because Christ bore the Father's wrath, we who believe in Him will never have to face sin's condemnation. What mercy! What love! And what grace! And all of these blessings are ours as followers of Jesus Christ!

The sacrifice of the Savior has set us free— free to do good and to enjoy the benefits of that choice; free to welcome death, knowing that when we enter the Lord's presence, we will face no judgment for sin, and free to enjoy the blessings of eternal life in an abode from which sin will be banished forever. Sin has been part of our lives for so long it is hard to imagine what it will be like to live sin-free, never having to watch what we think, say, or do ever again.

All people, however, will not be so blessed, the Bible tells us. Those who refuse to let Christ be their Sin-bearer, have made the choice to bear their sins themselves. And God will let them do just that. Throughout all eternity.

"You mean we're either in one camp or the other"? people ask. "There is no middle ground?" Let us see what God has to say in this matter. For *His* words are the words that matter.

Chapter 5

There Are Many Classes of People—or Are There Only Two?

"Whoever believes in the Son has eternal life, but whoever rejects the Son will not see life, for God's wrath remains on him."

—John 3:36

It is not unusual to think in terms of either-or. We either belong to the country in which we are living and enjoy the privileges of citizenship, or we are aliens with those privileges denied. When we go grocery shopping, we either have club cards that give us discounts on selected items, or we pay full price. When the pew registration form reaches us on a Sunday morning, we check either "church member" or "visitor" beside our names. No other option is listed except, perhaps, "interested in becoming a member."

With these contrasting illustrations in mind, it is not hard for us to understand the spiritual division the Scriptures make concerning where people are headed. They are either on the road to eternal life, or they are on the road to eternal death. There is no other road.

THE LORD'S CONCERN

God the Father showed concern for those on the road to eternal death when He addressed His own people, the Israelites in this way: *"The soul who sins is the one who will die...Turn away from your offenses. Why will you die...? For I take no pleasure in the death of anyone....Repent and live!"* (Ezekiel 18:20,30,32).

God the Son also showed concern for the lost. *"O Jerusalem, Jerusalem,"* the Savior lamented to the Pharisees, *"you who kill the prophets and stone those sent to you, how often I have longed to gather your children together, as a hen gathers her chicks under her wings, but you were not willing"* (Matthew 23:37).

Unfortunately, the majority of the Israelites paid little attention to their Sovereign's pleas. The same was true of the Pharisees. Are we surprised by their rejection of the Lord's overtures? We should not be. For people today react the same way. Consumed with their own interests, they seek their own glory and doggedly pursue it. A personal relationship with God is threatening to them.

God, however, is gracious to those on the road to destruction. He gives them the opportunity to come to Him. They can humble themselves, repent of their sins, and believe. The opportunity to change direction, however, will not last indefinitely. God's Spirit *"will not contend with man forever,"* the Bible warns (Genesis 6:3). One of these days the sovereign Lord will declare, "Enough is enough!" And the frightful destiny humanity deserves will be its everlasting portion.

A PAST EXAMPLE

People living in the days of Noah learned the cost of refusing to change course. *"The Lord saw how great man's wickedness on the earth had become,"* the Bible says, *"and that every inclination of the thoughts of his heart was only evil all the time. The Lord was grieved that he had made man on the earth,"* the Scriptures go on to say, *"and his heart was filled with pain. So the Lord said, 'I will wipe mankind, whom I have created, from the face of the earth...for I am grieved that I have made them'"* (Genesis 6:5–7). These words proved true. Only Noah and his family survived.

One of these days the Lord will again wipe the earth clean. Only this time the earth itself will be destroyed in the process. And the wrath sinful earthlings have *"stored up against themselves for the Day of Judgment"* will come upon them (Romans 2:5). As usual, people will blame God for their distress, but how foolish to do so when it is their own fault.

"Is my way unjust?" the sovereign Lord asked those who, in the past, questioned His judgment upon them. *"Is it not your ways that are unjust?"* (Ezekiel 18:25, emphasis added). You see, when God created life, He set up the law of cause and effect. This law dictates that people get what they earn. They reap what they sow. They pay for the choices they make. Either they pay for those choices themselves,

or they receive Christ's gracious invitation to let Him make sin's payment for them. It is an either–or situation.

Only Two Categories Of People

As we said earlier, God's two-category system of classifying individuals is pervasive in Scripture. The Word speaks of believers and non-believers, the saved and the lost, the repentant and the non-repentant, God's enemies and God's friends, doers of good and doers of evil. No third category is mentioned.

Such a clear-cut division rankles those who prefer distinctions that are fuzzy. These kinds of people like to think of salvation as coming in stages. If an individual has not rejected Christ outright, they reason, that person will receive God's blessing. After all, he/she is "closer" to the kingdom than downright infidels are.

In God's mind, however, no one is "almost saved." You are either in His kingdom, or you are not. You are either alive in Christ or you are dead in your sins (See Ephesians 2:1). And corpses are not usually rated as to which ones are more likely to start breathing. They are all in the same helpless state. Not one of them will come alive without a miracle. But God is in the business of doing miracles. Think of the grace He extended to each one of us. *"Like the rest,"* the apostle Paul said, *"we were by nature objects of wrath. But because of his great love for us, God, who is rich in mercy, made us alive with Christ even when were dead in transgressions—it is by grace you have been saved"* (Ephesians 2:4,5). God's grace, however, does not negate human responsibility. The apostle John noted, *"Whoever believes in the Son has eternal life, but whoever rejects the Son will not see life, for God's wrath remains on him"* (John 3:36).

HEADS IN THE SAND

Facing the wrath of God for ever and ever is such a horrible thought that people go into denial over it. They either refuse to think about it, dispute the fact that a place called hell exists, or rationalize their unbelief by saying, "The God of the Old Testament was a God of wrath, but I'm living in New Testament times. My God is a God of love. And a God of love would never send anyone to hell."

These reactions are dangerous. Refusing to think about the consequences of sin is folly. Denying that hell exists will not dematerialize it. And making two gods out of one cannot be supported by Scripture. The God of the Old Testament and the God of the New are one and the same (See Hebrews 13:8). Our sovereign Lord does not divide Himself in half. He is who He is—all the time, everywhere. He is a God of love *and* a God of wrath, a God of mercy *as well as* a God of justice, a God who shows kindness *along with* a God who can be severe. Hell is part of His severity. Sinners who reject Jesus Christ as their personal Savior and Lord are destined to spend eternity there, for hell is what Jesus died to save them from, and they have refused to appropriate His loving sacrifice.

"I'm going to live the best way I can," other folks say, "and hope that in the end God will be merciful to me." But how can God be merciful to people who reject the One through whom His mercy comes? Sin invites God's wrath. This wrath comes down upon either the sinner himself or upon Jesus Christ in the sinner's stead. Who bears the sinner's judgment is a choice the sinner gets to make. And that choice comes with consequences that are eternal. The Bible says, *"There is now no condemnation for those who are in Christ Jesus"* (Romans 8:1). But for those who are *not* in Christ Jesus there is *"a fearful expectation of judgment and of raging fire that will consume the enemies of God"* (Hebrews 10:27).

The fact that bad human choices have grave consequences is rooted in the very nature of God. It springs from who He is. God is just. That is why sin must be punished. God is holy. No impurity can enter His presence. And God is dependable; He keeps His word. When He says, *"he who pursues evil goes to his death,"* He means it (Proverbs 11:19). So the question is not whether unrepentant sinners will face eternal death; the question is, what kind of death will they face?

Consider Dying Eternally

In the last verse of Isaiah's prophecy, God's people are given a glimpse into the fate of evildoers. *"And they will go out and look upon the dead bodies of those who rebelled against me,"* the Lord says; *"their worm will not die, nor will their fire be quenched, and they will be loathsome to all mankind"* (Isaiah 66:24). From these words we learn several things about hell and how it affects those who are in it.

First of all, hell is everlasting. In the physical world, worms eat away at unpreserved dead bodies. In the case of bodies in hell, however, Isaiah is telling us that the *"worm"* will *"not die."* It will gnaw away at its prey forever. What this *"worm"* is, Scripture does not make clear. It may represent memory, for memories can come back to haunt the guilty. Or it may represent torment in general. Whatever it symbolizes, one thing is clear: in hell there will be no respite from punishment, no alleviation of pain, and no end to the suffering that is being experienced.

In the New Testament, Jesus goes on record as saying to those who reject Him, *"Depart from me, you who are cursed, unto the eternal fire prepared for the devil and his angels"* (Matthew 25:41). So we have evidence from both the Old and New Covenants that hell is eternal. No one assigned to it will ever be able to say, "Phew. It's over!"

Second, hell is darkness. Speaking of the Son of God, the Bible says, *"This is the verdict: Light has come into the world, but men loved darkness instead of light because their deeds were evil. Everyone who does evil hates the light, and will not come into the light for fear that his deeds will be exposed"* (John 3:19,20). Since evildoers love darkness, darkness is what they will get. And they will get it forever. Unfortunately, hell's darkness will not do for them what earth's did: cover their sin. Rather, hell's darkness will *"expose"* it (1 Corinthians 4:5). And with the exposure will come *"weeping and gnashing of teeth"* (Matthew 8:12).

Third, hell involves fire. Whether this fire is physical, spiritual, or a combination of both, it is very real. And it is something that can never be *"quenched,"* Scripture says

(Isaiah 66:24). Like the gnawing of the *"worm,"* its torment never ceases. Hell's fire must be something like that which enveloped Moses' *"burning bush,"* for there the flames kept licking at the branches, but the bush itself was never consumed (See Exodus 3:2). Hell's fire *"has been kindled by my wrath,"* the sovereign Lord says, and it is a fire *"that burns to the realm of death below"* (Deuteronomy 32:22). From it there is no escape. Ever.

Doctor Luke's account of the story of the rich man and the beggar Lazarus highlights the difference between eternal life and eternal death. *"The time came when the beggar died and the angels carried him to Abraham's side,"* Luke wrote. *"The rich man also died and was buried. In hell, where he was in torment, he looked up and saw Abraham far away, with Lazarus by his side. So he called to him, 'Father Abraham, have pity on me and send Lazarus to dip the tip of his finger in water and cool my tongue because I am in agony in this fire'"* (Luke 16:22–24).

The thought of unquenchable flames must have impacted Luke in a powerful way, for he is the only gospel writer to include this story. Perhaps it made such a strong impression upon him because, as a physician, he was charged with healing the human body, and what he was relating was the antithesis of healing. At any rate, as you read the story, you can almost hear Luke crying out with the Lord: *"Repent and live! Why will you die? Why?"*

Last, hell is separation from all that is good, holy, and true. When addressing the Thessalonian Christians, the apostle Paul put it this way: *"God is just: He will pay back trouble to those who trouble you and give relief to you who are*

*troubled....This will happen when the Lord Jesus is revealed
from heaven in blazing fire with his powerful angels. He will
punish those who do not know God and do not obey the gospel
of our Lord Jesus. They will be punished with everlasting destruction and shut out from the presence of the Lord and from
the majesty of His power on the day he comes to be glorified in
his holy people and to be marveled at among those who have
believed"* (2 Thessalonians 1:6–10, emphasis added).

What motivation to cry out to God for mercy, yet how
few do. The Bible prophesies that *"Multitudes who sleep in
the dust of the earth will awake: some to everlasting life, others
to shame and everlasting contempt. Those who are wise will
shine like the brightness of the heavens, and those who lead
many to righteousness like the stars for ever and ever"* (Daniel
12:2,3). The sovereign Lord said to the Israelites, *"I have
set before you life and death, blessings and curses. Now choose
life...."* (Deuteronomy 30:19).

What would it take to shake some folks out of their
spiritual complacency? I have often wondered. Would an
imaginary trip to hell do it? Would that convince them of
their spiritual folly?

I do not know, but just in case, I have included such
a "trip" in the following chapter. If you have a burden for
evangelism, consider performing the drama that follows
for your Bible class or for your church. Or consider sharing
the scripture verses that are part of the script with those
about whom you are spiritually concerned. Then pray that
God will use those verses for His glory—now and forever
and ever.

Chapter 6

A CRY FROM HELL
(A DRAMATIZATION OF
WHAT EVILDOERS FACE)

Place:	Hell: a darkened room (option: the audience closes its eyes)
Time:	Now
Characters:	1. A narrator, who reads the Introduction to the audience before the drama begins
	2. A woman, who becomes increasingly agitated as the dialogue progresses
	3. God, who speaks factually, omitting the Scripture references that accompany the verses He is quoting
Character positioning:	The woman and God deliver their lines from opposite ends of the room.

The Introduction

We live in an age when the love of God is being preached through every medium. Rightly so, for God is love. But God is also wrath. When we present His love at the expense of His holiness, we create a deity of our own imaginations. We make God out to be what we want Him to be, rather than accepting Him for who He is. So, the God we end up worshiping is not the one, true God. Also, by focusing exclusively on God's love, we lose an appreciation for the unimaginable horror His Son died to save us from.

In the Bible, God's love and His wrath go hand-in-hand. The sovereign Lord cannot embrace righteousness without rejecting unrighteousness. He cannot maintain purity by welcoming impurity. And He cannot remain holy if He tolerates even the slightest transgression.

As you might expect, God's holiness presents a problem to us sinners. It shuts us out of His presence. But God, in His love, made provision for our shortcomings. He planned a divine exchange. His Son took our sins and, in return, gives us His righteousness. This righteousness is our pass to life eternal.

What an amazing transaction that was! What an example of grace! Yet many fail to appreciate this grace. The reason may lie in their ignorance of God's wrath. For until we grasp the extent of God's wrath, we cannot appreciate the depth of His grace.

Therefore, the following dialogue has been prepared. It will transport us, via our imaginations, for one distasteful hour to hell. The purpose of this hour is three-fold. First, for all of us listening to this dialogue, regardless of our spiritual condition, it seeks to present God in His total majesty. Second, for those of us who have trusted Christ for personal salvation, it seeks to heighten our appreciation of what He suffered on the cross: the bearing of sins that were *ours*, the separation from God *we* deserve, the pangs of hell meant for *us*—all prompted by a love beyond comprehension. And third, for those of us who have toyed with Christianity without coming to a point of commitment, it seeks to lift up the Lord Jesus Christ, the One who still whispers, *"Come to me, and I will give you rest."*

In preparing this dialogue, it was necessary to take some literary license. Certain Scripture verses had to be lifted from their context and placed in the context of the dramatic presentation. We trust that the use of this license will heighten your appreciation of the implications of sin. Please notice that, except for two phrases, inserted and repeated for their theological significance, and for a change of pronouns in some cases, every time God speaks, He will be quoting Scripture as it is written.

He says to us, in preparation for what we are about to hear, *"Whoever believes in the Son has eternal life, but whoever rejects the Son will not see life, for God's wrath remains on him"* (John 3:36).

THE DRAMA

Woman: Where am I? It's so dark here. I've never been in such a dark place.

God: *"But the subjects of the kingdom will be thrown outside into the darkness, where there will be weeping and gnashing of teeth"* (Matthew 8:12).

Woman: Who said that? Who are you? Whoever you are, where are you? I can't see you. Speak, for God's sake, speak!

God: *"Who are you, O [woman] to talk back to God?"* (Romans 9:20).

Woman: God! God? O come on now, you're not God! But I'll play along if it'll make you happy. I mean, I've got to talk to somebody. So, now that I've made that concession, God, you make one: Answer my questions. Tell me why it's so dark. And tell me who's here besides me.

God: *"The cowardly, the unbelieving, the vile, the murderers, the sexually immoral, those who practice magic arts, the idolaters and all liars—their place will be in the fiery lake of burning sulphur. This is the second death"* (Revelation 21:8).

Woman: What do you mean by "the second death"? I haven't even died once yet, have I? Wait a minute! I remember something: a screech…a crash…pain… blood…darkness…it was awful. I don't want to talk about it. Are you telling me that's when I died—that now I'm dead…*dead?*

God: *"Dead in your trespasses and sin"* (Ephesians 2:1).

Woman: O come on, God, not "sins." That word went out
           with the Puritans. You'll never convince me I'm a
           sinner. I've never committed a crime in my life.

God: *"For all have sinned and fall short of the glory of
           God"* (Romans 3:23).

Woman: *"The glory of God."* Now that's a phrase I
           like...because my very existence brings glory to
           God...doesn't it? I mean I belong to the human
           race. I was created by God. Therefore, I am a
           child of God...aren't I?

God: *"You followed the ways of the world and of the ruler
           of the kingdom of the air, the spirit who is now at
           work in those who are disobedient...gratifying the
           cravings of [your] sinful nature and following its
           desires and thoughts...[you] were by nature [an]
           object of wrath"* (Ephesians 2:2).

Woman: An object of wrath! Come on, God, how could
           "sweet little old me" be an object of wrath?

God: *"Sin entered the world through one man and death
           through sin, and in this way death came to all men,
           because all sinned"* (Romans 5:12).

Woman: Sin entered the world through one man? When
           did that happen? Oh, don't tell me...not *"in the
           beginning"*?

God: *"In the beginning God created the heavens and the
           earth....God saw all that He had made and it was
           very good....The Lord formed the man from the
           dust of the ground and breathed into his nostrils
           the breath of life, and the man became a living be-
           ing....And the Lord God commanded the man, 'You*

are free to eat from any tree in the garden; but you must not eat from the tree of the knowledge of good and evil, for when you eat of it you will surely die' (Genesis 1:1,31;2:7,16,17). *The person who sins will die (and keep on dying and keep on dying)"* (Ezekiel 18:20 NAS).

Woman: But that's a myth. Nobody believes that anymore. I mean nobody with any education—people dying for simple disobedience...absurd! Completely absurd!

God: *"Just as Eve was deceived by the serpent's cunning, your mind [has been] led astray from your sincere and pure devotion to Christ"* (2 Corinthians 11:3).

Woman: Eve? The serpent's cunning? The mind's deception? That story's a joke. (Mocking): *"When you eat the fruit you will surely die."*

God: *"'You will not surely die', the serpent said to the woman. 'For God knows that when you eat of it your eyes will be opened, and you will be like God, knowing good and evil'"* (Genesis 3:4,5).

Woman: (Sarcastically) That must have been quite a deception to turn something *that* bad into something sounding that good. Quite a deception indeed!

God: *"Satan himself masquerades as an angel of light"* (2 Corinthians 11:14).

Woman: So? Suppose I believe your myth. What do Adam and Eve and Satan's deception have to do with me?

God: *"The result of one trespass was condemnation for all men"* (Romans 5:18).

Woman: Condemnation? I don't believe in condemnation. I don't believe in hell. Hell is a figment of the imagination. It doesn't really exist. God is a god of love. I've heard that all my life. He's not a god of condemnation.

God: *"There is now no condemnation for those who are in Christ Jesus"* (Romans 8:1).

Woman: *In* Christ Jesus? But I am *in* Christ Jesus, aren't I? I mean…I must be. I've done some pretty churchy things in the name of Christ Jesus: sung in the choir, sewn for the missionaries, baked for the bazaar, taught in the Sunday school, babysat in the nursery. Have I not in your name done many wonderful works?

God: *"I never knew you. Away from me, you evildoer!"* (Matthew 7:22)

Woman: Evildoer! You've got your nerve calling me an evildoer! Come on, God, be reasonable. They were *good* works that I did. They were done by a member of *your* church. I was a church member, you know. Remember all that ritual I sat through Sunday after Sunday? I have to admit: I didn't get much out of going to church. But I went. I sacrificed for you.

God: *"The multitudes of your sacrifices—what are they to me?"* (Isaiah 1:11)

Woman: Well, I thought they pleased you. Didn't they? Didn't you like the things I did for you? Take last Christmas. I decorated that entire church myself. You know I did: the trees, the wreaths, the incense. Didn't you like all that?

God: *"Stop bringing meaningless offerings! Your incense is detestable to me"* (Isaiah 1:13).

Woman: Well, forget the incense then. What about all those special services? You know…Easter, Christmas, Thanksgiving. I was always in my place on those holy days. Sometimes I even dragged my husband along. Didn't that please you?

God: *"New Moons, Sabbaths, and convocations—I cannot bear your evil assemblies. Your New Moon festivals and your appointed feasts my soul hates. They have become a burden to me; I am weary of bearing them"* (Isaiah 1:13,14).

Woman: Well, you may be weary of bearing them, but don't blame that on me. I thought you wanted those things. Take Lent. You know how much I dreaded it. But I endured it. I fasted for you. I fasted every year. Surely, God, you must want people to fast.

God: *"Although they fast, I will not listen to their cry; though they offer burnt offerings and grain offerings I will not accept them"* (Jeremiah 14:12).

Woman: Why not, God? Why not? Works, rituals, observances, fasting—they were sacrifices. And I made them. For You! I thought you wanted them. Good grief, God, what kind of sacrifices do you want anyway?

God: *"The sacrifices of God are a broken spirit, a broken and contrite heart"* (Psalms 51:17).

Woman: A contrite heart? Well, that's one thing I *know* I can offer you. I've got proof my heart is

right. Look how many times I took the Lord's
Supper.

God: *"Whoever eats the bread or drinks the cup of the
Lord in an unworthy manner will be guilty of
sinning against the body and blood of the Lord"*
(1 Corinthians 11:27).

Woman: Eats and drinks in an unworthy manner? How
dare you! I was sincere when I took Communion. How can you say I took it unworthily? I
took it as a Christian. I took it as one *"in Christ,"*
as you put it.

God: *"If anyone is in Christ, he is a new creation; the old has
gone, the new has come"* (2 Corinthians 5:17).

Woman: Exasperating! I can see I'll never win the argument this way! (Pause) Look...uh...God....Now,
I'm not admitting this, mind you, but let's just
suppose. Let's just suppose I never did become
a *"new creature,"* as you call it. Let's just suppose
Communion was only an external ritual for me.
You wouldn't damn me for that, would you?

God: *"Anyone who eats and drinks without recognizing
the body of the Lord eats and drinks judgment on
himself"* (1 Corinthians 11:29).

Woman: On himself? You're saying that I damned myself? And I did it by taking Communion? That's
ridiculous! What about my friends? They never
took Communion at all. Surely I am better than
they. They lived for themselves. They lived
in...uh... *"sin,"* as you call it.

God: *"You, therefore, have no excuse, you who pass
judgment on someone else, for at whatever point*

	you judge another, you are condemning yourself" (Romans 2:11).
Woman:	Condemning myself? That's the second time you've said that. And I don't like it. How could I condemn myself for judging others? Now I'm going to be honest with you, God. Let's suppose I did stumble once in a while. I mean, who doesn't? But most of the time I lived by a high set of standards. "Resolutions" I called them. I wrote them down one New Year's Day, word for word.
God:	*"By your words you will be acquitted and by your words you will be condemned"* (Matthew 12:37).
Woman:	Condemned by my own words? Condemned by my own standards? Condemned for taking Communion? Condemned for offering sacrifices? Condemned for doing good works? Can you tell me, please, how a list of what I would call "righteous activities" can condemn a person?
God:	*[God saves] not because of righteous things [you] have done, but because of his mercy. He [saves] through the washing of rebirth and renewal by the Holy Spirit"* (Titus 3:5).
Woman:	*"Renewal by the Holy Spirit, washing of rebirth"*—I remember hearing those words. They were emotional, fanatical, religious. I scoffed at them. I still do. I offered works instead. They were works of righteousness. I swear, they were works of righteousness.
God:	*"All [your] righteous acts [were] like filthy rags"* (Isaiah 64:6).

Woman: Filthy rags! Never! I won't accept that! When I
           was doing those works, I felt good. I felt I was
           really pure. Honestly, so help me God, when I
           was doing those works, I felt I was really pure.

God: *"To those who are corrupted and do not believe,
           nothing is pure. In fact, both their minds and con-
           sciences are corrupted"* (Titus 1:15).

Woman: Corrupted consciences? Corrupted minds? Are
           you telling me I can't even think straight? Well, if
           that's true, there must be none who escape your
           condemnation. Tell me, God, are there *any* who
           escape your condemnation?

God: *"Small is the gate and narrow the road that leads
           to life, and only a few find it"* (Matthew 7:14).

Woman: But how can *anyone* find it? I mean, if it's not by
           ritual, if it's not by sacrifice, if it's not by works,
           how can *anyone* find it? And don't tell me by
           the *"washing of rebirth."* I already heard you say
           that. I don't understand it. But this much I *do*
           understand: Washing has got to be something
           you do (if you really are God, of course). But
           I want to know what *people* do. Can *people* do
           anything to escape your condemnation?

God: *"Believe in the Lord Jesus and you will be saved"*
           (Acts 16:31).

Woman: *"Believe in the Lord Jesus, and you will be saved."*
           That's too easy. I can't accept anything *that*
           easy—at least not for stakes *that* high. But I've
           got to hand it to you, God. You've built yourself
           an airtight case. If I'm honest—and I am—I have

to admit I haven't done it—met your criteria for heaven, I mean. Not *my* criteria, mind you, but *your* criteria. I haven't met them. And neither have my friends. So, I'm going to ask you frankly, God: How come so many people fail to meet your criteria for eternal life?

God: *"The god of this age has blinded the minds of unbelievers, so that they cannot see the light of the gospel of the glory of Christ, who is the image of God"* (2 Corinthians 4:4).

Woman: The god of this age? Who's that? You mean...Satan? That "serpent" you mentioned before—the one who deceived Eve? Why, if that's true...and I don't believe it is...but if that were true, it would be the greatest deceit this world has ever known. I mean, Satan's not a person. He's a principle, an influence, a force. A force can't blind people's minds. I'm sorry God, but I don't buy that. When I was on earth, I determined my own destiny. *You* might not have been working in my life, but neither was Satan. Nobody influenced me. Nobody whispered in my ear. Whatever I've done—good or bad—I'll stand up and face. I'm a free moral agent, responsible for my own actions.

God: *"The person who sins will die (and keep on dying and keep on dying)"* (Ezekiel 18:20 NAS).

Woman: Come on now, God. One death is enough. I've already suffered that. And it's brought me here—to hell, as you call it. But hell doesn't exist. How can I be in a place that doesn't exist?

I must be dreaming. But why don't I wake up?
And why does it all seem so real? And why am
I so miserable?

(Silence)

(Vehemently) Cursed be this place! Damn this
horrible darkness! To hell with emptiness and
loneliness! "Hell" is a curse word. That's all it
is.Intelligent people don't believe in hell. Hell is
a myth!

(Silence)

But I'm in it. I'm in a myth! Absurd! Ridiculous!
I can't stand this. I've got to get out of here. Help!
Help me! Somebody help me!...Hey, you over
there in the dark, answer me. I know you hear
me. Why don't you answer me?

(Silence)

All right. Play the silence game if you want to. Is
that another technique you're using to condemn
me—your silence? I've got to admit, God, you're
pretty smart. You've hit a nerve. And you know
it. How can I argue with someone who doesn't
answer back? How can I win? I'm in a place that
isn't, but it sure seems real. I've argued why I
shouldn't be in this place that isn't, and not one
argument has been accepted. I've been asked to
accept statements that insult my intelligence,
and now this voice that calls itself "God" won't
answer anymore. He's left me to my thoughts.
And my thoughts frighten me. They tell me there
is a hell. They tell me there *is* a Satan. They tell

me faith in Christ, plus nothing, equals eternal
life. They tell me I ignored that truth.
(Argumentatively): Okay! So I did ignore it. Do
you want to know *why* I ignored it? I ignored
it because I hated it. I didn't understand it, but
I hated it: all that talk about Jesus, the goodie;
Satan, the badie; sin; blood; salvation. I couldn't
accept talk like that. I couldn't accept it when I
was alive. And I can't accept it now. Even if the
whole thing is true—and my reason is telling me
it's got to be—that doesn't alter my feelings. My
feelings are screaming in rebellion. I guess they
always will be. So, if this is hell, I'm in it. I guess
I deserve to be here. I sure couldn't be "there."
So I'm here—here forever, I'm told. And I can't
get out. O God, I can't get out! What am I going
to do?

(Silence)

Silent again, huh? (Pleadingly) Listen, God,
I've been honest with you. And I'm going to
continue to be honest, so please listen because
I'm not going to talk about myself. I'm beyond
help, I know that. I would need a new nature
to love in eternity what I hated on earth. So I'm
not asking for myself. I'm asking for my loved
ones, God—those who are still living. O God,
if the things you have told me are true, please
communicate that truth to my loved ones.
Dear God, they still have a chance to accept it.
They're still alive! They're still on earth! God,

help them. You've got to help them. There isn't anyone else. I mean, I'd tell them myself, but I can't get out of here. I'd even give my life to offer them escape, but I don't have it anymore to give. I'd suffer their punishment—willingly, but it looks like I'm going to have to suffer my own. I'm desperate, God. I love them: my husband, my kids, my parents, my friends. Dear God, I'd do anything for them. O God, I can't, but you can. You control things. Please, please, I beg you. Have somebody go tell them. I plead with you, God. I implore you. On behalf of my loved ones, please, send someone to my house, to my family, to my friends to warn them, so that they will not also come to this place of torment.

God: *"They have Moses and the Prophets [and the apostles, and the writers of the epistles]; let them listen to them"* (Luke 16:29).

Woman: They won't, God. They won't read the Bible. They won't read it any more often than I did. You've got to give them more than the Bible. You've got to give them more than words. God, send them a person. Send someone who's been here to tell them what it's like. If someone from the dead went to them, they would repent.

God: *"No. If they do not listen to Moses and the Prophets, [and the apostles, and the writers of the epistles], they will not be convinced even if someone [rose] from the dead"* (Luke 16:31).

Woman: *"Even if someone rose from the dead"*...O dear God!..."*Even though someone rose from the dead"*....Somebody did that, didn't He, God?

God: *"Christ died for [your] sins according to the Scriptures, [and] he was buried, [and] he was raised on the third day according to the Scriptures...Death has been swallowed up in victory"* (1 Corinthians 15:3,4,54).

Woman: (Resigned): Victory...that's a nice thought. But it has no relevance to my situation. *"Yours, [not mine], O Lord, is the greatness and the power and the glory and the victory and the majesty, for everything in heaven and earth is yours. Yours, O Lord, is the kingdom; you are exalted as head over all"* (1 Chronicles 29:11).

God: *"It is written: 'As surely as I live,' says the Lord, 'every knee will bow before me; every tongue will confess to God'"* (Romans 14:11).

Woman: I can't believe it! You know everything, don't you—even what I'm going to say before I say it. There are no surprises to you. Imagine! Knowing everything ahead of time, even that I would acknowledge your greatness and majesty! Why, I myself didn't even know I was going to do that. But I bet you enjoyed it, didn't you?

God: *"[This woman] honors me with her lips, but her heart is far from me"* (Mark 7:6).

Woman: There you go on the "heart" bit again. A change on the inside. Well, I can't make that change,

God. And you know it. You've won. You know
that, too. I have no other argument.

(Pause)

(Startled): What is that? It sounds like a trumpet.
But it can't be a trumpet. I mean, what would a
trumpet be doing in hell?

God: *"Blow the trumpet in Zion: sound the alarm on my*
holy hill...for the day of the Lord is coming...a
day of darkness and gloom...the earth shakes, the
sky trembles, the sun and moon are darkened, and
the stars no longer shine....The day of the Lord is
dreadful. Who can endure it?" (Joel 2:2, 10, 11)

Woman: Tell me what is happening, please. I can't see
anything, but you can.

God: (With pauses): *"I [see] the dead, great and small,*
standing before the throne, and books [are being]
opened. Another book [is being] opened, which
is the book of life. The dead [are being] judged
according to what they [have] done as recorded in
the books. The sea [is giving] up the dead that [are]
in them....Death and Hades [are being] thrown
into the lake of fire. The lake of fire is the second
death" (Revelation 20:11–14).

Woman: Death—I long for it, but it doesn't come. I want
to die, but I can't seem to make it happen. The
second death....I always thought death meant
things stopped. If this is death, then why doesn't
everything stop?

God: *"The person who sins will die (and keep on dying*
and keep on dying)" (Ezekiel 18:20 NAS).

Woman: What's that? What's that crackling? Who's that?
           Who's screaming? I can't see. What's happening?
           What's happening here?

God: *"Anyone whose name [is] not found written in the
           book of life [is being] thrown into the lake of fire"*
           (Revelation 20:15).

Woman: The lake of fire! Dear God, not that. Hell's a
           myth. It's got to be! Not me, God, no!

God: *"Depart from me, you who are cursed, into the
           eternal fire prepared for the devil and his angels"*
           (Matthew 25:41).

Woman: Fire that is eternal? Flames that last forever?
           God, I can feel them! My God, I can feel them! I
           can't see them, but I can feel them! God, how can
           this be: fire without light, fire in darkness? My
           God, these flames—they're following me! These
           flames, they're burning me! God, please kill me!
           Let me die. On earth flames bring death. But
           here, things are different. These flames, they're
           not consuming me. They're not burning me up.
           O God, when will this torment stop? When will
           it stop?

God: *"The person who sins will die" (and keep on dying
           and keep on dying)"* (Ezekiel 18:20 NAS).

Woman: Stop it! I can't stand to hear those words one
           more time. God, have pity on me and send some-
           body to dip the tip of his finger in water and cool
           my tongue because I am in agony in this fire.

God: *"[You] will be tormented day and night for ever
           and ever"* (Revelation 20:10).

Woman: But I can't stand it. God, I can't stand it. Being tormented forever is one thing. Being tormented *alone* is another. Remember what it was like on earth? There, people who suffered had company, and their company showed compassion. That's what I need, God: company, fellowship—somebody who will show compassion. Isn't there anybody around who still feels compassion?

God: *"Between us and you a great chasm has been fixed, so that those who want to go from here to you cannot, nor can anyone cross over from there to us"* (Luke 16:26).

Woman: I can't believe it. I just can't believe it: suffering but no compassion, multitudes of people but no one to keep me company, dying but no relief of death. And these flames—they're real. They're actually, literally real! I can feel them. They're engulfing me. They're tormenting me. God, they're tormenting me!

God: *"It's a dreadful thing to fall into the hands of the living God"* (Hebrews 10:31).

Woman: The *living* God. The *living* God. Those words are like cool water to my parched and dying throat: the *living* God.

God: *"I am the Living One; I was dead, and behold I am alive for ever and ever! And I hold the keys of death and Hades"* (Revelation 1:18).

Woman: Death, life! Dying, living! The contrast. I can't stand it. To be dying in the presence of the *living* God—dying, dying, always dying. Give me life! Give me life! Give me life!

God: "I am the resurrection and the life. He who believes
            in me will live even though he dies; and whoever
            lives and believes in me will never die (will never
            die, will never die)" (John 11:25,26).

God (to audience): "O unbelieving and perverse generation,
            how long shall I stay with you and put up with
            you?" (Luke 9:41)

            "I know you. I know that you do not have the love
            of God in your hearts" (John 5:42).

            "As surely as I live, I take no pleasure in the death
            of the wicked, but rather that they turn from their
            ways and live. Turn! Turn from your evil ways!
            Why will you die?" (Ezekiel 33:11)

            "For [I] so loved the world that [I] gave [my] one
            and only Son, that whoever believes in him shall
            not perish but have eternal life. For [I] did not send
            [my] Son into the world to condemn the world, but
            to save the world through him....Whoever believes
            in the Son has eternal life, but whoever rejects the
            Son will not see life, for [my] wrath remains on
            him" (John 3:15,17,36).

            "Surely as I have planned, so it will be, and as I
            have purposed, so it will stand" (Isaiah 14:24).

            "And you will know that I am the Lord"
            (Ezekiel 6:7).

            Amen.

Part Two

Situations to Scrutinize: Evil in Bible Times

"For everything that was written in the past was written to teach us, so that through endurance and the encouragement of the Scriptures we might have hope."

—Romans 15:4

Chapter 7

EXCESSIVE EVIL IN NOAH'S DAY AND GOD'S RIGHTEOUS JUDGMENT

"The Lord saw how great man's wickedness on the earth had become, and that every inclination of the thoughts of his heart was only evil all the time."

—Genesis 6:5

Up to this point we have been pondering the theology of evil: its power, its origins, its submission to God's will, its influence upon human nature, and the cost it exacts from those who choose to let it dominate their lives. Now we want to concentrate on some instances of evil in the Scriptures to see how God dealt with them. To introduce our first example, let me ask you a question: Do you ever wonder what it might have been like to be a TV reporter in the days of Noah? What events would you record? Whom would you interview? How would you present your story?

The first place you and your camera crew would go, undoubtedly, would be to the site where, according to rumor, an "ark" was being constructed. Positioning yourself amidst stacks of lumber, close enough to the activity to catch the sound of pounding, you would set out to interview a few onlookers.

"He's crazy!" one man shouts toward the camera, as you go move the microphone toward his mouth. "Old man Noah is crazy!"

"He hears voices," a woman contributes. "He thinks God is talking to him."

"Look at this thing he's building!" an engineer exclaims, gesturing wildly. "Take in the size of it! Count the number of compartments!"

"Noah thinks humanity is going to be punished for its sins," a young man explains. "He says water is going to fall from the sky and come up from the depths of the earth, drowning everybody who's not in his 'ark.' Have you ever heard anything more ridiculous?"

You decide to approach the "madman" himself. "I'm building this structure in faith," Noah offers, putting his hammer down. "God says this earth has become so evil there is no alternative but to destroy it. I have a holy fear of my Maker, so when He warns me of impending doom, I believe Him. I just wish everybody else would believe Him, too, because if they don't, they are going to die!" (see Hebrews 11:7).

For your next stop, you and your camera crew decide to go into town. You want to determine how great an influence Noah's preaching has had on the public at large. The New

Testament says, *"For in the days before the flood, people were
eating, and drinking, marrying and giving in marriage, up to
the day Noah entered the ark; and they knew nothing about
what would happen until the flood came and took them away"*
(Matthew 24:38,39). After asking a few questions and taking a few camera shots (one of couples having lunch at a
sidewalk café, another of a Justice of the Peace conducting
a wedding ceremony, and a third of several men entering a
brothel), you tell your viewing audience, "As you can see,
in this town at least, it's business as usual. There's no fear
of divine judgment here."

Uh Oh!

One day, however, raindrops start falling from the sky.
Up to this point the earth has been watered by gentle mists,
(see Genesis 2:6 KJV). So, when large droplets appear, and
they begin descending in quantity, people become fasci-
nated. Your cameraman takes a picture of children with
faces uplifted, and palms outstretched. He takes shots of
adults too, looking heavenward, jaws gone slack.

Fascination quickly turns to fear, though, when the rain
starts coming down in torrents. The ark, with Noah, his
family, and a host of animals inside, is slowly being lifted
off its foundation. You position your microphone near the
structure's bottom so your viewers can hear the creaking
of the wood. You provide a running commentary as the ark
begins to float.

Then the earth beneath you starts convulsing. Water
begins spouting from breaks in the crust. You and your

crew scramble for higher ground, but soon there is no more higher ground on which to flee. Suddenly your electrical power shorts out, and with it goes your broadcast. You realize your imagined days as a journalist in Noah's time are over. You awaken from your reverie troubled.

Was there screaming as the water engulfed its victims? Were mockers cursing Noah for his predictions? Did some pound their fists on the side of the ark in frustration? Were any crying to be let inside? You will never know.

Moses, when recording the account of the flood, spared his readers these details. So did the authors of the New Testament. But one of them, Matthew, made an interesting observation. He saw a connection between the evil that existed in Noah's day and that which will plague society right before the return of Jesus Christ. *"As it was in the days of Noah,"* he wrote, *"so it will be at the coming of the Son of Man....Therefore, keep watch, because you do not know on what day your Lord will come"* (Matthew 24:37,42). There is timeless truth, as well as rich symbolism, in the historical account of Noah and his trustworthy ark.

CHRIST, OUR ARK, NOW AND ALWAYS

According to the Bible, the story of Noah is more than a historical record of events. In it lies applications that are contemporary. Just as in Noah's day the earth was exceedingly wicked, so is the earth in our day. Just as Noah's society deserved God's judgment, so does our modern one. And just as Noah obeyed God and found refuge in the ark, we too can obey God and find refuge in the Lord Jesus Christ. *"God* is our refuge and strength, an ever-present help in trouble," the psalmist asserts. "Therefore, we will not fear," he continues, "though the earth give way and the mountains fall into the heart of the sea, though its waters roar and foam, and the mountains quake with their surging" (Psalms 46:1–3).

There are other applications as well. As God shut the door to the ark once Noah and his family had boarded (Genesis 7:16), so He protects believers until the new world they will inhabit is ready to receive them. As nothing harmful was permitted to enter Noah's ark, nothing will be allowed to separate believers "from the love of God that is in Christ Jesus [their] Lord" (Romans 8:38,39). And as divine retribution follows human wickedness, so will it be in our day, sooner or later. "If [God] did not spare the ancient world when he brought the flood on its ungodly people," the apostle Peter wrote, "but protected Noah, a preacher of righteousness and seven others.... if this is so, then the Lord knows how to rescue godly men from trials, and to hold the unrighteous for the day of judgment, while continuing their punishment" (2 Peter 2:5,9).

The above Scripture passage makes two promises: 1) God will provide a sanctuary for the "godly" in times of trouble, and 2) God will punish the "unrighteous" for their sins. Actually, both of these promises contain comfort. The first assures us that when life comes in like a flood, we Christians have an ark we can run to for shelter. The second relieves us of the burden to inflict upon our enemies the justice that is due them. When we are mocked for our faith, tested for our endurance, or subjected to such personal indignities as Noah was, God does not look the other way.

He sees to it that all injustices are avenged, either here or in the hereafter. In Noah's day it was "here."

Natural Disasters and God's Righteous Judgment

God made it clear to Noah that it was He, the Lord, who was behind the cataclysmic event that took the lives of many, many people. *"I, even I, do bring a flood of waters upon the earth,"* He told Noah, emphasizing the word "I" (Genesis 6:17 KJV). By so doing, He was saying, "Although I am the First Cause behind everything that happens on the earth—First Cause in the sense that I make decrees to bring about, either directly or indirectly, all things that take place in My world (See Ephesians 1:11)—in this case, Noah, I am going to intervene in nature and move directly, causing a huge flood. This flood will be My response to the widespread sin that is polluting My earth."

Why did God use a natural disaster as a judgment in Noah's day? For the answer, we turn to Genesis, chapter 6, verse 5, the passage quoted at the beginning of this chapter. Man was *wicked*, God tells us there. His wickedness on the earth was *great*. The inclinations of his heart were *evil*. *Every* inclination of his heart was evil. Every inclination of his heart was *only* evil. Every inclination of his heart was only evil *all the time* (emphases added)! From these emphases it is hard not to get the picture. Cause and effect were at work. Man's willful disobedience brought on God's righteous judgment. This is how God had set up his moral

order, and this is how that moral order was playing out in
Noah's day.

In biblical history, if God brought about a natural disaster to serve as either a punishment or as a corrective
discipline, He made sure the people got the connection.
For example, in Moses' day, when the earth suddenly split
apart and swallowed Korah, Dathan, and Abiram, God told
the people why the earthquake happened. These men had
treated Him *"with contempt,"* He said (Numbers 16:30).
They deserved what happened to them.

In Abraham's day, when *"the Lord rained down burning
sulphur on Sodom and Gomorrah"* (Genesis 19:24), He made
sure both Abraham and Lot knew why the city was being
destroyed. It was because of sin (See Genesis 18:20,21;
19:12,13).

In Jonah's day, when the waves arose and the ship Jonah
was on was about to break up, the prophet told the sailors,
"I know it is my fault that this great storm has come to you"
(Jonah 1:12). Jonah's disobedience had triggered the squall,
and he knew he was its cause.

In the days of Amos, the Lord made the following statements: *"I gave you empty stomachs in every city and lack
of bread in every town...,"* (4:6). *"I also withheld rain from
you when the harvest was still three months away..."* (4:7).
*"Many times I struck your gardens and vineyards; I struck
them with blight and mildew..."* (4:9). Mark the repetition
of the personal pronoun in each of these statements. God
wanted His people to know He was the One behind their
problems. He also wanted them to know their problems
were the result of their sin.

Does this mean, then, that *all* natural disasters are God's judgment on sin? No. Although all natural disasters are the result of sin in general—sin related to the Fall—this does not mean that all natural disasters are necessarily linked to the specific sins of specific people, committed at specific times in their lives. On the contrary, the earth may simply be *"groaning as in the pains of childbirth,"* waiting to be delivered from its bondage (see Romans 8:22). In this respect, it resembles the human body, which also *"groans"* to be set free.

Having said this, however, I hasten to add that a natural disaster *could* be an act of God's judgment, even in this present age. So, it is not out of order to ask, "Are you trying to tell us something, Lord?" If He is, I think we will know it. God will "speak" to us, either through a *"gentle whisper,"* as He spoke to Elijah after the prophet had experienced wind, earthquake, and fire (See 1 Kings 19:12) or more directly, as in the case of Noah.

THE RESPONSIBILITY OF SPECTATORS

Trying to discern God's intentions in tragedies as they affect us personally is one thing. Thinking we know His intentions in regard to others who are experiencing tragedies is something else. Was the Asian tsunami a judgment? What about the devastating U.S. hurricanes? What about the huge earthquake in Pakistan? It behooves us to be careful here. We all know that the person who points an accusing finger at others ends up having three fingers pointed back toward himself.

Jesus warned about the danger of drawing conclusions that could be false. Are we Christians presuming to know the mind of God? When a tower in Jerusalem fell, killing eighteen people, Jesus asked His disciples, *"Do you think [the people who died] were more guilty than all the others living in Jerusalem?* (Luke 13:4). The obvious answer was, "Of course not. All people are guilty. All people have sinned. It is because of God's mercy that all of us are not consumed *'every morning'"* (Lamentations 3:22,23).

On a more positive note, it helps to remember that God can work through disasters to bring sinners to Himself. So, if the victim of a tragedy feels God is trying to get his/her attention, maybe He is. Seeing God's hand in a disaster can lead to conviction of sin. And conviction of sin, in turn, can lead to salvation. It can also lead believers to closer fellowship with the Lord. When Joseph of old recognized God's involvement in his misfortune, personal victory came. The same thing happened to Job. To be blessed afresh by the stories of these two godly men, read on.

Chapter 8

How Evil Targeted Joseph and Job and How God Used It for Good

"They sharpen their tongues like swords and aim their words like deadly arrows. They shoot from ambush at the innocent man; they shoot at him suddenly, without fear."
—Psalms 64:3,4

When I was a young girl, I was privileged to attend summer camp. While there, I had the opportunity to develop new skills. One was with the bow and arrow.

During my first archery class, we beginners were introduced to our equipment. There were wooden bows with strings drawn tight, wooden arrows with metal tips at one end and real feathers at the other, and a round, straw target on a stand. The target was covered with canvas that had been stamped with colorful, concentric circles. Hitting the yellow bullseye in the center would score the most points.

After becoming familiar with the tools, we were anxious to learn how to use them. Position yourself properly, take careful aim, and release your arrow gently, we were told. When it came my turn to shoot, the instructor was hovering over me. Nervously, I secured my arrow, lifted my weapon, turned sideways, and aligned my eye with the bullseye. At this point I hesitated. Immediately the instructor placed his hands over mine, pulled back on the string, and kept my hand steady as I released the arrow. *Bam!* It hit—not too far from where I was aiming.

Years later, after I had became a teacher of the Bible and had discovered the biblical phenomenon that God uses all actions, even evil ones, for His own good purposes, I thought of that first archery lesson. I knew I harbored no evil, and I knew that both the instructor and I were aiming at the same target. However, I wondered about the result of my shot. Would it have turned out as well if the instructor had not put his hand over mine? With that question in mind, I chose to study two men of the Bible whom I knew to be "targets" of evil intentions: the patriarchs Joseph and Job. Would the pain they experienced have made them better people if the Lord had not guided every "arrow" that attacked them? I looked at Joseph's life first.

TARGET: JOSEPH

Joseph, you will remember, was next to the last son of Jacob, the Hebrew progenitor of the twelve tribes of Israel. Joseph's father had entrusted him with a position of family leadership and had given him an elaborate robe signifying

his special status. His brothers resented this display of fa-
voritism, and their resentment is what prompted them to
try to hurt him. The arrows came.

Blow #1: Joseph's siblings kidnapped him and sold him
to traveling merchants. The young man ended up in Egypt
in the service of a palace guardsman named Potiphar.

Blow #2: One day Potiphar's wife tried to seduce Joseph;
and when Joseph refused her advances, she had him thrown
into prison.

Blow #3: While incarcerated, Joseph made friends with
a fellow inmate who happened to be the king's cupbearer.
The cupbearer promised to put in a good word for Joseph
once he gained his freedom. Unfortunately, the cupbearer
forgot his pledge.

God, however, did not forget Joseph. In time the Lord
reminded the cupbearer of the vow he had made in prison.
The cupbearer, then, mentioned Joseph's plight to the Egyptian monarch, and Joseph was set free. Eventually Joseph, an
interpreter of Pharaoh's dreams, was elevated to a position
of second-in-command over all of Egypt.

Some time later a famine, foretold in one of Pharaoh's
dreams, spread throughout the land. Joseph prepared for
it by putting away surplus grain during the years of plenty.
He stored away so much, in fact, that there was enough to
share with neighboring peoples when the need arose.

One day Joseph's brothers arrived in Egypt to purchase
some of this grain. Joseph took advantage of the occasion
to reveal his identity to these men, who years before had
sinned against him. It was a poignant moment. *"And now
do not be distressed and do not be angry with yourselves for*

selling me here," he explained to his brothers, *"because it was to save lives that God sent me ahead of you"* (Genesis 45:5). Later Joseph would say to them, *"But as for you, you thought evil against me, but God meant it unto good…"* (Genesis 50:20, KJV).

So, whose hand guided the brothers' poisoned "arrows" toward Joseph? I asked myself. According to the verses we just read, God's hand did. The sovereign Lord used human agents, sinful though they were, to bless His servant Joseph and to save His people from starvation.

Actually, I saw that God guided *all* the arrows that afflicted Joseph, not only his brothers', but Potiphar's wife's and the cupbearer's as well. The Lord's hand was always on top, directing the hurtful actions of his human agents to targets different from the ones they were aiming at. Whereas the human agents, for the most part, had evil in mind; God had good. In the end, God was the One who scored the winning points, and, as we said before, Joseph and the Israelites ended up receiving the blessings.

Target: Job

Next, I turned my attention to Job. As I did so, I wondered if the two patriarchs had anything in common. I discovered that they did. First of all, both men were respected by those who knew them. In Joseph's story Pharaoh is recorded as saying, *"[T]here is no one so discerning and wise as you"* (Genesis 41:39), and Job is introduced in the beginning of his biography as being *"blameless and upright,"* a man

who *"feared God and shunned evil"* (Job 1:1). I concluded I
was studying the lives of two men of integrity.

Second, both men became targets of evil unwittingly, I
learned. They were not anticipating the blows they received,
and from the human point of view they did not deserve
them. Since I had already examined Joseph's "hits," I now
turned my attention to Job's.

Blow #1: Marauders stole Job's oxen and donkeys.

Blow #2: Lightning struck Job's sheep, killing not only
his animals but most of his servants as well.

Blow #3: Raiding parties swept down on Job's camels
and carried them off.

Blow #4: As if these blows were not enough, Job then
received the hardest one of all: *"Your sons and daughters
were feasting and drinking wine at the oldest brother's house,"*
a messenger told him, *"when suddenly a mighty wind swept
in from the desert and struck the four corners of the house.
It collapsed on them and they are dead...."* (1:19). One can
only imagine Job's pain at learning he had lost all ten of his
children, but more blows were to come.

Blow #5: *"Satan afflicted Job with painful sores from
the soles of his feet to the top of his head,"* the Bible says
(2:7). Now Job's body, as well as his emotions, was being
targeted.

Blow #6: Job's wife, driven perhaps by frustration over
the events of the past few days, challenged her husband to
renounce this God to whom she was attributing her pain.
In her mind, Job probably would be struck dead for cursing
the Lord. With him gone, maybe her own troubles would go
away. Job, however, refused to curse God. Instead, he said

to his wife, *"What? shall we receive good at the hand of God, and shall we not receive evil?"* (2:10 KJV). With this tribute to God as First Cause of all things, tragedies too, some harm from blow #6 was avoided, but there were more blows to come, this time from supposed "friends."

Blow #7: Eliphaz, Job's Temanite friend, came to offer comfort but ended up making accusations instead. *"As I have observed,"* Eliphaz pontificated, *"those who plow evil and those who sow trouble reap it"* (4:8). In other words, "You're getting what you deserve, my friend. These troubles have come upon you because you've sinned." Reeling from this smack, Job tried to defend himself, but then came…

Blow #8: Bildad, Job's Shuhite friend, chimed in by saying, *"Surely God does not reject a blameless man or strengthen the hands of evildoers"* (8:20). He meant, "You are not a blameless man, Job. You are evil. That's why God has rejected you and has refused to help you." Again Job offered a defense. Then came…

Blow #9: Zophar, Job's Naamathite friend, picked up his own poisoned arrow and aimed it straight toward the heart. *"Surely [God] recognizes deceitful men,"* Zophar said, *"and when he sees evil, does he not take note?"* (11:11). For a third time Job put up his defenses. In his pain, however, Job's defenses became a mixture of questioning the God he had refused to curse and acknowledging Him as the Benevolent One in control of all that happens in the world. *"I will wait for my renewal to come,"* Job resolved as this first round of exchanges came to an end (14:14). It was a triumphant assertion of Job's reliance upon his Redeemer in the midst of circumstances that appeared to be overwhelmingly evil.

Unfortunately, Job's three friends delivered a second round of blows. This round included more references to Job's being evil (see 15:16,35;18:21;20:12). This time Job turned the accusations being made against him back toward those who were doing the shooting. As he did so, however, he was careful to acknowledge God's sovereignty. *"God has turned me over to evil men and thrown me into the clutches of the wicked,"* he said (16:11).

Then came a third round of exchanges. Again there were accusations (22:15). On one thing Job decided to agree with his accusers: courting evil is never a good thing. *"The fear of the Lord—that is wisdom,"* he acknowledged, *"and to shun evil is understanding,"* (28:28). But then he admitted, *"[W]hen I hoped for good, evil came; when I looked for light, then came darkness"* (30:26). Who of us cannot identify with Job's bewilderment over his plight? I certainly found myself doing so.

GOOD FROM EVIL

When evil attacks, it is natural to resist, at first at least, to become defensive, to argue one's innocence. Sometimes, however, it is better to let God do the fighting, I realized from reading these men's stories. As far as Joseph was concerned, the Lord was with him, the Bible says, every step of the way (see Genesis 39:2,3,21,23). The same was true of Job. Long before the two men realized it, God was busy working out a master plan for each of their lives. By trusting that God *did* have a plan and by surrendering to it, whatever it was, the two Hebrews learned patience, trust, forgiveness, and many more valuable lessons as well.

Job's story was more complex than Joseph's, I realized, for Satan was much more actively involved in his troubles. It seems that during one of God's accountability sessions for His angelic messengers (1:6), the Lord asked Satan to consider His servant Job, a man with whom He was especially pleased. Satan countered by attributing Job's good behavior to the fact that God had placed a protective *"hedge"* around him (1:10). *"But stretch out your hand and strike everything he has,"* Satan said, *"and he will surely curse you to your face"* (1:11).

To prove to Satan that Job trusted the Lord in all things, God placed Job and his possessions in Satan's hand (see Job 1:8–12, 20–22; 2:3–10). There were limitations to Satan's activities, but that did not seem to bother the evil one. He got to work immediately, aiming his stinging arrows straight toward his human target. He shot some of his arrows directly, such as when he inflicted Job with a devastating disease. And he shot some indirectly, using people and nature to cause Job's pain. By using a storm, Satan was trying to make it look as if God were punishing Job as He punished the evil people in Noah's day when, in fact, the storm in Job's case was not a judgment at all. It was something the sovereign Lord was using to test and to strengthen His servant's faith.

In the end, *"the Lord made [Job] prosperous again,"* the Bible says, *"and gave him twice as much as he had before"* (42:10). But most of all, Job, like Joseph, was blessed spiritually through his ordeal. He gained a new understanding of God (42:5), a new understanding of himself (42:6), and a prominent place in biblical history (see James 5:11). A believer committed to making his life count for eternity can not ask for much more than this, I concluded.

It helped that Job had his theology right. *"Far be it from God to do evil,"* Job said at one point. *"It is unthinkable that God would do wrong"* (34:10,12). Yet Job, like Joseph, knew that God could use evil to accomplish ends that were holy, so he submitted to whatever it was God wanted to do, albeit at times reluctantly. *"The arrows of the Almighty are in me,"* he recognized (6:4). Then came the submission: *"Though he slay me, yet will I trust Him"* (13:15 KJV). These are words repeated in Christian circles even today as a testimony to Job's faith and perseverance in times of darkness.

Through the stories of these two men, I learned that believers in the sovereign Lord have nothing to fear from any and all "arrows" that come their way, whether those arrows are from God, from Satan, from demons, or from other humans; for God uses all the wounds of His followers to bring about ends that are good. For people who are not followers of the sovereign Lord, however, there is no guarantee that *anything* will turn out good. Think of king Saul. What a disaster his life turned out to be! How can we avoid the pitfalls that snared him? we ask. We will pick up some pointers in the following chapter. Please turn the page.

Chapter 9

KING SAUL'S EVIL SPIRIT FROM THE LORD: A POSSIBLE EXPLANATION

"Now the Spirit of the Lord had departed from Saul, and an evil spirit from the Lord tormented him."

—1Samuel 16:14

My friend Judy and I were welcoming neighbors to our weekly Bible study. When Juanita walked in, she looked concerned. After we all took our seats, we found out why. "In my devotions this morning," Juanita exclaimed, "I read that king Saul had an evil spirit that came from the Lord. An evil spirit *from the Lord?*" she asked, her voice rising with every syllable. "How can there be such a thing? I mean, I thought God was good. How in the world can something bad come from a God who is good? How can an evil spirit come *from the Lord?*"

People all over the world are wondering about the connection between a God who is good and things that are bad, I thought. *Juanita is asking a question that is universal. Answering it, however, will sidetrack our study. What should I do?*

I sneaked a look at our hostess Judy. Her eyes said, "Go for it!" So I did. What I explained—or tried to explain that Friday afternoon—probably went something like this:

IMPRESSIVE BEGINNINGS

King Saul was a sick man. No question about it. If he were living in our day, he probably would be diagnosed with schizophrenia or bipolar disorder. His attending physician, would probably prescribe antipsychotic and/or mood-altering drugs. These drugs, however, would do little to alleviate Saul's problem, the root of which was sin. The king had given himself over to evil. And this evil was tormenting his soul.

Few who knew Saul, however, could have predicted his problems. Early impressions of the youth were glowing. He was *"an impressive young man without equal among the Israelites—a head taller than any of the others,"* the Bible says (1 Samuel 9:2). When his father asked him to track down some lost donkeys, Saul took a servant with him, as advised, and began his assigned task with diligence. There is not a hint of rebellion. When Saul could not find the lost animals in a reasonable amount of time, he said to his servant, *"Come, let's go back, or my father will stop thinking about the donkeys and start worrying about us"* (1 Samuel 9:5). He seemed to be sensitive to what his father might be feeling.

Young Saul also displayed humility. When the prophet Samuel told him that God had big plans for him, he answered, *"But am I not a Benjamite, from the smallest tribe of Israel and is not my clan the least of all the clans of the tribe of Benjamin?"* (1 Samuel 9:21). Later, when Saul was about to be presented as Israel's first king, he hid, the Bible tells us, shunning public adulation (1 Samuel 10:22).

The young man manifested other commendable qualities as well. When a group of malcontents refused to bring any gifts to his coronation party, *"Saul kept silent,"* the Bible says (1 Samuel 10:27b). Later, when the king was advised to put these rabble-rousers to death, he decided instead to spare their lives. Self-control and compassion had joined the list of Saul's attributes.

Shortly after his inauguration, King Saul faced a test of his leadership. It seems the Ammonites were besieging the city of Jabesh Gilead and, in the process, were frightening the Israelites into a quick surrender. When King Saul heard of the peace-at-any-price treaty his people were about to make with the enemy, he was furious. *"The Spirit of God came upon him in power,"* the Bible says, *"and he burned with anger"* (1 Samuel 11:6).

He went out, slaughtered some oxen, and purposely cut them up. Then he traveled throughout the area, depositing pieces of the animals' rotting corpses in strategic places. This was a warning of the division that would occur if God's people did not band together and fight—a division that would bring a stench to the nostrils of the sovereign Lord.

The illustration worked. The people united behind their new king, rallied the troops, and attacked the Ammonites. They came forth victorious. As a result, their confidence in Saul soared.

WHAT WENT WRONG?

Unfortunately, the virtues that Saul demonstrated in his early years got eclipsed by the evil in his heart. Let me give you two examples of his sin nature breaking through. One involved impatience. It seems that the prophet Samuel had agreed to meet the king at a designated place. When the prophet arrived, he, the prophet, would make a required sacrifice to the Lord. When Samuel did not show up in what Saul considered to be a reasonable amount of time, the king performed the religious ritual himself (see 1 Samuel 13:9). The problem was, Saul had been anointed to perform kingly duties, not priestly ones. In the eyes of God, his action was a serious offense. People in the past had been struck dead for such presumption. Who did Saul think he was?

On another occasion, the king disobeyed a divine order to destroy the spoils of war. God's instructions had been to annihilate everything associated with the Amalekites. In this way Saul would be acting as God's instrument of justice on a nation that was evil (see 1 Samuel 15:3).

The king, however, failed to do as he had been told. Instead of destroying *everything*, he decided to destroy *some* things. He was sparing *"the best,"* he said, keeping them for a sacrifice to the Lord, (1 Samuel 15:15). Confronted with his sin, Saul lied, three times in fact. But to keep up appearances, he made sure to perform an act of worship in front of the nation's elders.

SIN'S CONSEQUENCES

It was after this incident that three unfortunate things happened to Saul: God's Spirit departed from him, David was anointed to take Saul's place, and the deposed king began to be tormented by his *"evil spirit from the LORD"* (1 Samuel 16:14). So it appears that Saul's evil spirit was the result of his own evil doings: a consequence of his many transgressions against the Lord.

The fact that Saul's troubles were of his own making, however, does not rule out demonic involvement. The Bible calls Saul's spirit "evil." Since this term is usually associated with things originating in the *"dominion of darkness"* (Colossians 1:13) and since the Bible tells us that *"the devil prowls around like a roaring lion, looking for someone to devour"* (1 Peter 5:8), it is logical to assume that on those occasions when Saul was being tormented, the devil or one of his underlings was attacking him, *"devouring"* him, as the Scripture says, turning him into a despondent, irrational, even vengeful human being, who would try to murder his successor and would end up killing himself.

In his later years, Saul seems to have given in to the darker side of life. Remember his encounter with the witch of Endor (1 Samuel 28)? Anxious to learn how a pending battle with the Philistines would turn out, Saul unwisely

116 · Making Sense of Evil

consulted a medium, and he did so knowing he was in the wrong. The Hebrew Scriptures contained a warning against meeting with fortune tellers. *"Let no one be found among you who...engages in witchcraft, who is a medium or spiritists, or who consults the dead,"* Deuteronomy clearly states (18:10,11). To his credit, the king had made an effort to expel all *"mediums and spiritists from the land"* (1 Samuel 28:3). But then he found himself consulting one who had escaped the purge. Clearly, he was a man of conflicting purposes.

Whether or not Saul's fascination with the occult opened him to attacks of Satan—attacks that would result in periodic bouts of depression—the Bible does not say. (Saul's encounter with the witch of Endor occurred *after*, not before, his debilitating angst took over.) The fact that the Bible attributes Saul's oppression to a spirit that is *"evil,"* though, indicates there may have been more to the king's problems than just personal disobedience. Demons may have oppressed or even possessed him.

What Role Did God Play?

Since the Bible says King Saul's evil spirit was *"from the Lord,"* where does *"the Lord"* fit into this picture? it is natural to ask.

Actually, there are several places in Scripture where evil spirits, lying spirits, spirits of delusion and the like are associated with God. We will look at one of them now, hoping it will shed some light on Saul's problem. Turn with me to Judges 9:23, if you will. As we read this section of God's

Word together, we will discover that the arrival of an evil spirit in this particular case was a judgment on sin. But let me give you some background information first. It seems that Abimelech, a ruler of the Israelites during the age of the judges, had duped the citizens of Shechem into helping him murder his brothers who were rivals to the position of power he was coveting.

God was angry with the way Abimelech had gained leadership, so He turned those who had helped Abimelech against him. *"Then God sent an evil spirit between Abimelech and the men of Shechem,"* the Bible says, *"and the men of Shechem dealt treacherously with Abimelech"* (Judges 9:23, NAS). God did this, the Scriptures continue, *"in order that the crime against Jerub-Baal's seventy sons, the shedding of their blood, might be avenged on their brother Abimelech and on the citizens of Shechem, who had helped him murder his brothers."*

The citizens of Shechem ended up fighting against Abimelech in a battle Abimelech won, but when the leader went to destroy another city in the same way he had destroyed Shechem, a woman climbed a tower and with great accuracy dropped a millstone on Abimelech that cracked his skull. *"Thus God repaid the wickedness that Abimelech had done to his father by murdering his seventy brothers,"* the Bible says (Judges 9:56).

This story brings to mind the New Testament admonition that *"God cannot be mocked. A man reaps what he sows. The one who sows to please his sinful nature, from that nature will reap destruction..."* (Galatians 6:7,8). If the *"reaping"* comes through a God-sent evil spirit, as it did in the cases of Abimelech and King Saul, so be it. God has access to, and authority over, every part of his created world. Evil spirits are no exception. As Martin Luther said, "The devil is God's devil!" Indeed he is.

In Saul's case, after he had been anointed king, he heard Samuel say to the people, *"If you fear the LORD and serve and obey him and do not rebel against his commands, and if both you and the king who reigns over you follow the LORD your God—good! But if you do not obey the LORD, and If you rebel against his commands, his hand will be against you, as it was against your father"* (1 Samuel 12:14,15). Saul knew this warning included him, yet he made a conscious choice to disobey it. As a result, God sent a spirit from the realm of evil to judge him for his deliberate and willful sin. The spirit was not the Lord, and the Lord was not the spirit. But the Lord has the right to use any spirit for His own ends and purposes. That is what He did with king Saul. Thus we have the phrase, *"an evil spirit from the LORD."*

No Jumping to Conclusions!

This explanation does not mean, of course, that all depression and melancholy are God's punishment for personal wrongdoing. On the contrary, those of us in the more technically advanced part of the world know that mental and emotional disorders can be chemical in nature. They can be treated—and often treated successfully—with modern medications.

The above explanation also does not mean that a personal disorder can never turn into a blessing. Actually, *anything* can become a blessing for those who are repentant of their sins and seeking to stay in close fellowship with their Lord. King Saul, however, chose not to be in this category. He had reached a point where fellowship with the Lord was something to be shunned. By thinking this way, Saul had put himself in a dangerous position.

We learn later in the Bible that the king's unfaithfulness to his calling, coupled with deliberate disobedience, especially in *"consulting a medium for guidance,"* cost him his life and his kingdom (1 Chronicles 10:13,14). Sin carries a high price tag, does it not? And it is the sinner who does the paying. He pays regardless of who or what might have influenced him, for he is one hundred percent responsible for his own willful actions. That is why when punishment comes, it is just. That is why no one can say, "That's not fair!" There are rules in this game of life. Break them and you end up in the penalty box. Keep them and your soul prospers. God is holy and never unjust.

GOOD FROM EVIL

Because of the amazing grace of God, several blessings for God's people came out of King Saul's sins. His disappointing conduct prepared the Israelites to receive a better monarch: King David. King David, in turn, became the forerunner of the ultimate monarch, King Jesus. In Saul's story we see selfish ambition, dark designs, and purposes that are destructive. But we also see a redemptive plan that is capable of taking all these negative forces and using them to bring about a grand and glorious future.

It is good for all of us that God acts redemptively, be-cause every one of us needs His hand upon our actions, making sense of the messes we have made. Israel's second king, King David was no exception. Although there is little to compare between King Saul and King David, the second king had his own problems with sin. In the next chapter, we will reexamine some events in the life of King David, reminding ourselves that when someone truly repents, God is there to forgive.

It is too bad King Saul did not realize this, for he could have been forgiven too. The Lord's forgiveness is there for anyone who wants it, the Bible says. It is a spring of fresh water running through a world filled with filth and corrup-tion. If we but step into this refreshing stream, He will wash even "the foulest" of us clean. King David *did* step in.

Chapter 10

KING DAVID'S FLIRTATIONS WITH EVIL AND GOD'S GRACIOUS FORGIVENESS

"Have mercy upon me, O God....Against you, you only, have I sinned and done what is evil in your sight, so that you are proved right when you speak and justified when you judge."

—Psalms 51:1,4

I t was springtime in Jerusalem—the season when kings lead their soldiers in military expeditions. David was Israel's ruler, but he had not joined his troops in battle. On this particular night, he was at home, relaxing on the flat roof of his luxurious palace. Suddenly he caught sight of a beautiful woman. She was bathing. He sent for her, she came to him, the two slept together, and the woman ended up getting pregnant.

Now what? David was married. So was Bathsheba, the object of his lust. She was the wife of Uriah the Hittite, an officer in King David's army. Her husband, though a mercenary, was a disciplined soldier known for his loyalty. He would be outraged if he knew his wife had been violated.

King David panicked. He needed to find a way to cover his sin. But how? *Ah ha! Why not call Uriah home for an evening and get him to sleep with his wife? Then when she announces she is pregnant, Uriah will assume the baby is his.* It sounded like a foolproof idea.

But would it work? The king sent a summons to the officer, and the officer came to his palace. So far so good. But when it was suggested the officer might want to sleep in his own bed that night, he said he could not pamper himself in that way. After all, his men were camping out in open fields. So Uriah spent the night with the king's servants, sleeping near the palace gate.

Did the officer suspect something? We do not know. What we do know is that David was persistent. His scheme had to work! Under pressure, the king asked Uriah to spend one more day in Jerusalem—a request with which the officer dutifully complied. On this second evening king David got Uriah drunk. Perhaps the alcohol would nudge the soldier toward his waiting wife. No luck. Again Uriah placed his mat among those of the palace servants, and once more he slept beside the palace entrance.

Frustrated, the king reached a decision point. He would have to get rid of Uriah any way he could! As James points out in his New Testament epistle, it is amazing how quickly temptation leads to sin and sin leads to death (See James 1:13–15). In this case, it would be physical death—the death of Uriah.

David dashed off a letter calling for Uriah's demise and addressed it to Joab, his field commander. And—get this—he had Uriah deliver the letter! Joab read the letter and quickly complied with his written instructions. He placed Uriah in the front lines of battle, commanded the other soldiers to withdraw, leaving the officer exposed, and then watched as this dedicated military man drew enemy fire and fell. *Mission accomplished!* David thought.

AN UNEXPECTED CONFRONTATION

The king had covered his sin. At least he thought he had. Now it was time to do something magnanimous. In the Hebrew culture, you will remember, it was customary for recent widows to be taken under someone's protective care. So David *"brought Bathsheba to his house,"* the Bible says, *"and she became his wife and bore him a son"* (2 Samuel 11:27). By marrying the widowed Bathsheba, the king was presenting himself as a model citizen and a compassionate monarch. However, what the people thought about him and what God thought were two different things. *"[T]he thing David had done displeased the Lord,"* the Bible says. King David had not been successful in hiding his sin after all, at least not from the eyes of an omniscient God.

He also could not hide his sin from himself. The guilt he experienced was so intense it made him sick. Listen to David's words of anguish as he expressed them to the Lord: *"Because of your wrath there is no health in my body; my bones have no soundness because of my sin. My guilt has overwhelmed me like a burden too heavy to bear. My wounds fester and are loathsome because of my sinful folly. I am bowed down and brought very low; all day long I go about mourning. My back is filled with searing pain..."* (Psalm 38:3–7).

How long the king battled this psychosomatic illness we do not know. But at some point he pleaded for God's forgiveness. *"Have mercy on me, O God,"* David cried, *"according to your unfailing love; according to your great compassion blot out my transgressions. Wash away all my iniquity and cleanse me from my sin. For I know my transgressions and my sin is always before me. Against you, you only, have I sinned and done what is evil in your sight..."* (Psalm 51:1–4).

God's forgiveness came to David, as it comes to all who are repentant of their sins. And the change it made in his physical condition, to say nothing of his spiritual condition, was astounding. Listen to David's words following his confession: *"Blessed is he whose transgressions are forgiven, whose sins are covered....When I kept silent, my bones wasted away through my groaning all day long. For day and night your hand was heavy upon me; my strength was sapped as in the heat of summer. Then I acknowledged my sin to you and did not cover up my iniquity. I said, 'I will confess my transgressions to the Lord'—and you forgave the guilt of my sin...."* David then concludes, *"[T]he Lord's unfailing love surrounds the man who trusts in him"* (Psalm 32:1–5,10).

A CONFRONTATION

How did David come to the point where he was willing to confess his sin and be forgiven? The catalyst was a confrontation by the prophet Nathan, who was quite creative,

I believe, in the way he pointed out David's transgression. He told the king a story about a rich man who had many sheep and a poor man who had only one; this "one" was the family pet. When a traveler arrived at the rich man's property, tired and hungry from his day's journey, the wealthy host decided to prepare a meal of mutton. Unfortunately, instead of selecting a lamb from his own flock, he took the poor man's single lamb, a family pet, and killed it.

At this point in the story David got incensed. *"The man who did this deserves to die!"* he shouted to Nathan. *"He must pay for that lamb four times over…"* (See 2 Samuel 12:1–6).

"You are the man!" Nathan said, pointing an accusing finger at the king. Then he explained how God had given the king everything he could possibly want and yet the king had coveted what somebody else had. In fact, the king was so consumed by desire he would even commit murder. *"Why did you despise the word of the Lord by doing what is evil in his eyes?"* Nathan asked David. Then he prophesied what would be the consequences of the monarch's evil actions. You see, in God's economy, even though a sin has been forgiven, earthly consequences follow. God has built into the moral structure of life the principle of cause-and-effect.

A HEAVY PAYMENT

In King David's case, because the king had lain with a woman who was not his wife, someone else would lie with *his* wives, the prophet predicted—and do so *"in broad daylight before all Israel"* (2 Samuel 12:12). Because David had

Uriah killed by the sword, Nathan continued, the sword *"would never depart"* from David's house. Both of these prophecies, harsh as they were, would come to pass exactly as God's spokesman had predicted.

But the worst consequence of all came as a fulfillment of David's own words: *"He must pay for that lamb four times over!"* Although this was the judgment the king had pronounced on the heartless rich man in Nathan's story, it was David, not the fictional rich man, who would end up making the payment. And he would do so with the lives of four of his sons. The first victim was his son by Bathsheba, who died shortly after birth (2 Samuel 12:18). The second was Ammon, killed by Absalom in retaliation for raping his sister Tamar (2 Samuel 13:32). The third was Absalom, who conspired to wrest the kingdom from his father and ended up getting killed by field marshal Joab (2 Samuel 18:14). And the fourth was Adonijah, who was slaughtered by an order from King Solomon, another son of David by Bathsheba and successor to King David's throne (1 Kings 2:25).

These payments were heavy ones, and they caused the monarch much grief. During his ordeal David's only consolation was the knowledge that he was a forgiven man. This assurance got him through his pain. It did not, however, cancel it. The only way to cancel the anguish that follows an act of evil is to avoid that evil in the first place. If David had thought about the consequences of his sin ahead of time, a lot of people would have been spared heartaches, himself included.

DAVID'S OTHER BIG SIN

Most Christians know about King David's sin with Bathsheba. Fewer are acquainted with his other notable transgression—ordering a census to be taken of Israel's fighting men. From the human point of view, counting troops seems like a reasonable thing to do, especially when one is facing a serious battle. In the eyes of God, however, this deed indicated a reliance on human power instead of on divine enablement. It was, to God at least, another deed that was "*evil*" (See 1 Chronicles 21:7).

It appears the devil made David do it. "*Satan rose up against Israel and incited David to take a census of Israel,*" the Bible says (1 Chronicles 21:1). In another place, however, it says "*...the anger of the Lord burned against Israel, and HE incited David against them saying, 'Go and take a census of Israel and Judah'*" (2 Samuel 24:1 emphasis added). So who was responsible for the idea to number the troops: God or Satan? And what role did David himself play?

According to the Bible, David, like Joseph's brothers, Job's accusers, and King Saul before him, acted without manipulation or coercion. After the census was completed, David was so overcome with guilt, he made this forthright confession: "*I have sinned greatly in what I have done. Now, O LORD, I beg you, take away the guilt of your servant. I have done a very foolish thing*" (2 Samuel 24:10). Please notice that if David knew about the roles Satan and God had played in the troop numbering, he did not mention it. As far as he was concerned, he was the one who had done the deed. So, the consequences of the sin were his to bear. Right on,

David! You can not be forgiven by God if you do not take ownership of what you have done.

The Lord's "ownership" of David's sinful action, however, is another matter. It begs a question: Why would the Lord incite David, albeit through Satan, to do something sinful—something for which He would later punish him? Well, for one thing, the Lord wanted to discipline Israel, and Israel's king was the instrument He was planning to use to bring on the punishment. God can use evil, you will remember, without robbing the human of his freedom in committing that evil. He can also use evil to accomplish purposes that are holy and good. He can even use evil without becoming tainted by it. We have seen evidence of this phenomenon several times in our study. We have also noted that God's good use of a bad thing does not make that bad thing good. Nor does it excuse the sinner for doing it. It simply shows who is in control. And that is the sovereign Lord. Every time. We know all these things, but it is still difficult to see how they fit together.

The best we can do in this case, I believe, is to say that God moved through Satan, who, in turn, moved through David, who, in turn, did an evil deed that ended up accomplishing purposes that were holy. In the process, Israel was punished for its transgressions, David was chastised for his sin, Satan's schemes were used by God and God was glorified in all of it.

THE APPLICATION

What can we learn from David's sins? The first lesson is this: it is dangerous to flirt with evil. We can save ourselves a lot of heartache by simply saying no when temptation comes. Second, never is it wise to cover one sin with another. This practice will boomerang in the end. Third, keep short accounts with the Lord, confessing each transgression as soon as it happens. And when God forgives, appreciate the grace you have received. God's pardon is something not to be taken lightly. After all, it cost Him the life of His Son to offer it.

The Israelites, God's chosen people, made that very mistake; they took God's pardon lightly. To them it was a license to sin, and they used that license again and again. They failed to see evil for what it is, an assault on the holy nature of the sovereign Lord. To teach them how offended He is when His people deliberately sin, God did an amazing thing; He used evil to punish evil. If you want to see just how He accomplished this feat, continue reading. The chapter that follows is one of the most fascinating of all.

Chapter 11

USING EVIL TO PUNISH EVIL: GOD'S UNIQUE PREROGATIVE

"Therefore the Lord Almighty says this: 'Because you have not listened to my words, I will summon all the peoples of the north and my servant Nebuchadnezzar, king of Babylon…, and I will bring them against this land and its inhabitants and against all the surrounding nations…, and these nations will serve the king of Babylon seventy years. But when the seventy years are fulfilled, I will punish the king of Babylon and his nation, the land of the Babylonians, for their guilt…. I will repay them according to their deeds and the work of their hands.'"

—Jeremiah 25:8–14

Using evil to punish evil, then holding the doers of the evil responsible for the sins they committed in the process—only God could orchestrate such a phenomenon! And on occasion, He did just that, as the above Scripture passage indicates. But the Lord, it seems, resorted to such a measure only when sin had become so vile there seemed to be no other alternative.

Because God's people had been singularly blessed, they were held to a high standard of holiness. They had been chosen of all the peoples of the world, you will remember, to be custodians of the law, ancestors of the Redeemer, and role models of how a blessed people are expected to react when delivered from bondage. They were provided for abundantly, protected in times of trouble, encouraged when depressed, forgiven when repentant, empowered when weak, and led miraculously across the river into the Promised Land.

Unfortunately, they failed miserably in these responsibilities. Think back. Remember how the Israelites mocked the Lord, refused to obey His commands, and engaged in practices the Lord called *abominable*? Let me highlight for you some of the Israelites' more *detestable sins*. I will do so with the humble realization that we Christians do not do much better when it comes to resisting the powers of evil.

IN THE WILDERNESS

The Israelites had no sooner escaped the pursuing Egyptian army then they started grumbling against their leader Moses. The first thing that annoyed them was Moses' command to make camp at Marah where the water proved to be undrinkable. Although God took care of the problem by detoxifying the water (See Exodus 15:25), the restless mob was mollified only for a while. Soon, they were back to bickering again.

"*[You] have brought us out into this desert to starve this entire assembly to death,*" they complained (Exodus 16:3). This charge, of course, had no foundation, and to prove it God provided in another miraculous way. He rained down bread from heaven. The falling manna served to fill their empty stomachs, but it did not satisfy their cravings. "Give us meat, give us meat, give us meat!" they nagged.

"OK," God said after their wailing reached a feverish pitch, "if you want meat, I will give you meat. '*You will not eat it for just one day, or two days, or five, ten , or twenty days, but for a whole month—until it comes out your nostrils and you loathe it'*" (Numbers 11:19).

The prophecy came to pass in a most unusual way. The Lord sent in quail from the sea—so many quail, in fact, that at one point the fallen fowl measured three feet deep (v 31). The Israelites, throwing caution to the wind, gathered up these fallen birds and gorged themselves. Many got sick. Some died. What did they learn from this lesson?

Nothing. When the wandering multitude stopped again, it was at a location where there was no oasis. Instead of relying on the Lord, who had already proved Himself to be an adequate Provider, they grumbled, "*Why did you bring us up out of Egypt to make us and our children and livestock die of thirst?*" (Exodus 17:3). "*Strike the rock,*" the Lord told Moses, "*and water will come out....*" Moses did so, and the people's thirst was quenched. But there was a critical spirit inside some of them that simply refused to be quieted.

This critical spirit manifested itself again when the Lord was giving the Ten Commandments to Moses on Mt. Sinai. While they were waiting for their leader to return, the Israelites took off their jewelry, melted it in a fire, and fashioned a golden calf like the idols they had seen in Egypt. The inevitable followed. They began offering sacrifices to this pagan god and began indulging themselves in sinful revelry.

When Moses came down from the mountain, stone tablets in hand, he was enraged at what he was witnessing. He was so angry, in fact, that *"he threw the tablets out of his hands,"* the Bible says, *"breaking them to pieces at the foot of the mountain"* (Exodus 32:19). God's judgment was quick and sure. Three thousand Israelites fell by the sword, we are told, and a plague claimed the lives of many more. Did God's people shape up after this incident?

No. As the multitude approached the Promised Land, some of the people became fearful about going in sight unseen, so they asked Moses to send spies ahead to check it out. Moses did so, and a favorable report came back. God's people, however, gave little credence to what the spies had told them. They had convinced themselves that they were not powerful enough to overcome the *giants* currently inhabiting the land. Their lack of trust made the Lord so angry He proclaimed, *"Not a man of this evil generation shall see the good land I swore to give your forefathers except Caleb...and Joshua"* (see Deuteronomy 1:19–46). This was another prophecy that came to pass. But there was still no change in the Israelites' bent to sin.

The Israelites came in contact with the Moabites, who were living near the Jordan River. These people worshiped Baal, a son of the fertility goddess Asherah. In order to get Asherah to bless them, they engaged in prostitution at designated religious shrines, located on *high places*. These heathen practices lured some of the Hebrew men, and before long, God's leaders began to *"indulge in sexual immorality with the Moabite women,"* the Bible says (Numbers 25:1). This sin made the Lord so angry He exclaimed to Moses, *"Take all the leaders of these people, kill them, and expose them in broad daylight"* (v 4). This harsh sentence was implemented. Twenty-four thousand people died, the Bible says. Unfortunately, the toll sin took that day still was not sufficient to stop the Israelites from flirting with evil. It makes one wonder if *any* judgment, however severe it might be, will stop a people who are determined to sin.

IN THE PROMISED LAND

Once the Israelites crossed the Jordan, they had to fight battles to make the Promised Land their own. The first was the battle of Jericho. Their obedience to God's instructions during this fight was exemplary, and it paid off. They won. After the battle, however, evil tempted them. You see, God had commanded the Israelites to destroy everything—absolutely everything—in the city they had just conquered. They were to take no spoils whatsoever. Achan disobeyed this injunction and took some of the enemy's treasures, hiding them in his tent. Because he coveted what God had cursed, he, his family and his livestock were stoned to death, and their bodies were burned (See Joshua 7:25). It was not a good beginning in the land God's people had anticipated possessing for forty long years.

The people did settle down, however, and over time "judges" arose to become their rulers. Under the leadership of these "judges," a disturbing sequence of events emerged. The Israelites would willfully commit sins that God said were grievous (See Judges 3:7), and God, in His mercy, would let the people enjoy their sins for awhile. Then He would step in and put them under the oppression of a foreign tyrant. (This oppression is an example of God's using evil to punish evil.) When the Israelites finally realized there was a connection between their sin and the oppression they were experiencing, they would repent of their wrongdoing and cry out for mercy. The sovereign Lord, then, would send a "deliverer," and Israel would be saved from its misery (See Judges 3:31). Sin, judgment, repentance, deliverance—this sequence became a pattern of life for these rebellious Israelites; and it repeated itself over and over again—to the dismay of their longsuffering Lord.

Things got worse during the age of the kings. To see how bad it became, it helps to back up a bit. You will remember that when the Israelites were still on the other side of the river, God had said to them, *"When you cross the Jordan into Canaan, drive out all the inhabitants of the land before you"* (Numbers 33:51). *"[D]estroy them totally. Make no treaty with them, and show them no mercy....Break down their altars, smash their sacred stones, cut down their Asherah poles, and burn their idols in the fire"* (Deuteronomy 7:2,5). Although these instructions might seem stringent to readers unfamiliar with the religious practices of the Canaanites, to those who have studied these practices, there was no alternative but to do what God had commanded. You see, the Canaanites, like the Moabites, engaged in pagan ritualistic prostitution. This practice often produced pregnancies. The resulting infants, then, were *"passed through the fire,"* the Bible says. This phrase is a euphemism for "were sacrificed to the pagan god Molech, another son of the fertility goddess Asherah." In other words, the babies were burned alive on Molech's altar. The only way to stop this detestable practice was through a purge. Everything had to go—people, livestock, altars, Everything! *"If you do not drive out the inhabitants of the land,"* God continued, *"those you allow to remain will become barbs in your eyes and thorns in your side"* (Numbers 33:55).

The Israelites did *not* drive out all the inhabitants of the land, as they had been instructed. And they did *not* totally destroy the cities they conquered. As a result, they got ensnared by the evil they allowed to remain. The decline of their love for God was gradual, as leaving one's first love often is; but where it ended up was astounding. Not only did God's people engage in the worship of false deities in practices God called *"abominable"* and *"detestable,"* but they also brought these pagan practices into the temple of the Lord, into the very place that was dedicated to the One True God. It was Manasseh, King of Judah, who led the Israelites into this syncretistic worship. *"He did evil in the eyes of the Lord,"* the Bible says, *"following the detestable practices of the nations the Lord had driven out before the Israelites"* (2 Kings 21:1–9).

LATER ON

In the years that followed, the evil God's people participated in was off the chart. It included lies, murders, briberies, rapes, conspiracies, betrayals, sorceries, prostitution, idol worship, human sacrifice, and even cannibalism. Earlier, you will remember, God had used the Israelites to punish the Canaanites. Now it was time for God to punish the Israelites, who had become even worse than the Canaanites. (To the Lord, mixing the false with the true seems to be more abominable than following the false alone.) He would rather have His people *"cold"* or *"hot"* than in between, or *"lukewarm,"* as the apostle John aptly puts it (Revelation 3:15,16).

The Lord's instrument of judgment upon Israel, the Northern kingdom, was Assyria, the cruel superpower of the day. *"[A]ssyria is the rod of my anger,"* God said, *"in whose hand is the club of my wrath. I send him against a godless nation* (Israel); *I dispatch him against a people* (Israel) *who anger me..."* (Isaiah 10:5,6). Then God goes on to explain, *"But this is not what* [Assyria] *intends. This is not what* [Assyria] *has in mind;* [Assyria's] *purpose is to put an end to many nations....I will punish the king of Assyria for the willful pride of his heart and the haughty look in his eyes"* (v 7).

Did you get that? God is saying He will use evil Assyria to punish evil Israel, whom He has already used to punish evil Canaan. Then He will punish evil Assyria for the impure motives in its heart. Only God could be so creative in using evil to punish evil to punish evil and be just and right in doing so. It is an amazing study.

God did something similar with Judah, the Southern Kingdom. *"Because you have not listened to my words,"* God said to Judah, *"I will summon...my servant Nebuchadnezzar, king of Babylon....This whole country (Judah) will become a desolate wasteland....But when the seventy years* (of captivity) *are fulfilled, I will punish the king of Babylon and his nation, the land of the Babylonians, for their guilt....I will repay them according to their deeds"* (Jeremiah 25:8–14).

To Babylon the Lord said, *"I gave* [Judah] *into your hand and you showed them no mercy....Now then, listen, you wanton creatures, lounging in your security.... Disaster will come upon you"* (Isaiah 47:6,8,11). To Judah the prophet Isaiah said, *"The Lord's chosen ally* (the Chaldeans) *will carry out his purpose against Babylon; his arm will be against the Babylonians"* (Isaiah 48:14).

Here it is again. God is repeating with the Southern Kingdom what He did with the Northern. God is saying He will use the Babylonians to punish the Israelites; then He will use the Chaldeans to punish the Babylonians. All three nations were involved in blatant evil, we must remember, and all three got exactly what their evil actions deserved. Since God is the First Cause of everything that happens, He has the prerogative of using secondary causes, even evil ones, to highlight righteousness and to punish unrighteousness.

Being "First Cause," you will remember, does not mean God is the Author of evil. Given His holy nature, this is an impossible and unthinkable prospect. But God *is* the Author of how evil is used. Listen to how the Reverend James Loveland, pastor of Community Baptist Church in

Neptune, New Jersey, explains the phenomenon: "God as First Cause 'wills' or 'decrees' to use evil. He is kept separate from the evil because He does not 'touch' it or 'move' it to do what He wills. Rather, He sovereignly 'decrees' what is to happen and it is accomplished. He does this without being the 'active Agent' or 'Doer.' God created the natures of those He uses—demons and sinners—and provides the situations in which the evildoers find themselves. But they themselves commit the evil acts, freely choosing to do what their evil wills dictate. In so doing, they not only accomplish what their evil, sinful natures eagerly desire, but they also accomplish the sovereign Lord's decrees!"

A QUESTION

When God used evildoers to chasten His people, you may be asking, did any good come from it? Yes it did. A *"remnant"* of true believers came through the furnace of affliction *"refined"* (See Isaiah 48:10). There is nothing like suffering to make one *"strong, firm, and steadfast,"* the apostle Peter says (1 Peter 5:10). In suffering God has a plan for His own—a plan that is healing and good. That plan is always accomplished.

Thankfully, those of us on this side of the cross do not live under the Old Covenant, which warned, "Obey or die." Rather, we are under a New Covenant, which promises, "Believe and live." However, we can never take our gift of grace lightly. There are evil forces in *our* lives, too, waiting to devour us as surely as they devoured the Israelites. Can we handle these evil forces on our own? No way. But we have a

God who can. Will His solution be effective? Absolutely—as effective as it was for the Israelites, who, at one point in their wilderness journey were plagued with an abundance of poisonous snakes and got miraculously cured. Keep on reading to see what God did in that case.

Chapter 12

THE TRIUMPH OF GOOD OVER EVIL, SYMBOLIZED BY A SNAKE

"Just as Moses lifted up the snake in the desert, so the Son of Man must be lifted up, that everyone who believes in him may have eternal life."

—John 3:14,15

We were walking through the woods with several of our grandchildren. Suddenly a snake slithered across the path in front of six-year-old Ethan. He reached out to touch it. We stopped him. "Snakes can be dangerous," we cautioned. "You have to be careful around snakes."

How true. From the beginning of time, snakes have been associated with evil. The Bible testifies to this fact. It was a serpent, you will remember, that tempted Eve in the Garden of Eden, luring her to commit the very first sin (Genesis 3:13). Later, when Moses and Aaron went before Pharaoh of Egypt to plead for the deliverance of the Hebrews, they encountered sorcerers, who, like they themselves, could turn rods into snakes. The powers of evil, however, met their match in the powers of God when, as the Bible says, *"Aaron's staff swallowed up* [the sorcerers'] *staffs"* (Exodus 7:11,12). It was an encouraging victory.

Further on in the Bible, we see king David likening deceit to *"the venom of a snake"* (Psalms 58:4). In another psalm, the writer tells the reader, *"You will tread upon the lion and the cobra,"* meaning, you will overcome things that are out to harm you (Psalms 91:13). Still further in God's Word the prophet Isaiah says that the Philistines looked upon King Uzziah, their oppressor, as a *"viper"* and King Hezekiah, his successor, as a *"darting venomous serpent"* (Isaiah 14:29). And the prophet Amos, when warning God's people of judgment to come, verbalized his alarm in these words: *"It will be as though a man...entered his house and rested his hand on the wall only to have a snake bite him"* (Amos 5:19). Yes, snakes in the Old Testament are connected with evil.

In the New Testament the same thing is true. When John the Baptist saw some Pharisees and Sadducees coming to watch him baptize repentant believers, he cried out, *"You brood of vipers! Who warned you to flee from the coming wrath? Produce fruit in keeping with repentance"* (Matthew 3:7). Jesus later referred to these religious hypocrites in the same derogatory way.

When giving his Sermon on the Mount, Jesus used the metaphor again, this time to show people what He would *not* give them when they prayed. *"Which of you,"* He queried, driving home his point, *"if his son asks for bread will give him a stone? Or if he asks for a fish will give him a snake?"*

Later He told his disciples that in sharing the gospel, they would need to be *"as shrewd as snakes and as innocent as doves"* (Matthew 10:16). And when He sent them out two by two, He told them, *"I have given you authority to trample on snakes and scorpions and to overcome all the power of the enemy; nothing will harm you"* (Luke 10:19).

Further along in the Bible, we read that when the apostle Paul was bitten by a snake on the island of Malta, the people at first thought the bite was God's judgment on an evil man; but when Paul showed no effects of his bite, they changed their minds and called him a god (see Acts 28:1–6). In the book of Romans, when Paul was describing unregenerate mankind, he said, *"The poison of vipers is on their lips"* (Romans 3:13). And in the last book of Holy Writ, Satan is referred to as *"that ancient serpent…who leads the whole world astray"* (Revelation 12:9). So, snakes and evil go together from the beginning of God's Word to the end.

SNAKE WORSHIP

The association of snakes with things sinister is true in other religions as well. Yet because of the power attributed to snakes, early humankind started worshiping them. *"Although* [the unregenerate descendents of Adam] *claimed to be wise, they became fools and exchanged the glory of the immortal God for images made to look like mortal man and birds and animals and reptiles,"* the Bible says. *"They exchanged the truth of God for a lie, and worshiped and served created things rather than the Creator—who is forever praised….Therefore, God…gave them over to a depraved mind, to do what ought not to be done"* (see Romans 1:18–28).

There is evidence of this *"depraved mind"* in culture after culture, ritual after ritual. In ancient Egypt, there was a god named Apepi, who was represented as a giant serpent. This god chased the sun god Ra through the heavens, at times causing solar eclipses.

In ancient China there was an abundance of serpents and dragons. Likenesses of these creatures were embroidered on clothing, carved into the backs of chairs, sculpted in stone, painted on porcelain, and displayed on posters. The Chinese celebrated a period of time called The Year of the Snake. They still do.

In Central America, the Mayans incorporated snakes into their architecture. They worshiped the monkey god of the underworld, which they represented with a snake slithering out of its mouth. And they carved, among other things, the statue of a Mayan priest holding a scepter in the form of a serpent.

In the ancient ruin of Angkor Wat in Cambodia, there are snakes everywhere, I am told. The snake is also worshiped in India. The Aztecs of Mexico, the Incas of South America, and some of the North American Indians also revered snakes. Today, if you are in the right place at the right time, you may be able to watch the re-enactment of an authentic Hopi Indian snake dance. And if you should take the time to visit a museum and look through the various symbols that early Native Americans used, you might notice the picture of a snake. It is associated with "defiance and wisdom," you will read. (Back to Eden anyone?)

Consult Greek mythology and you will read about Hydra, a snake with nine heads. You will also learn of Medusa, who had protruding fangs for teeth and writhing snakes for hair. Roman mythology, which borrowed heavily from the Greeks, seems to have added a few snake deities of its own. It came up with the Roman Furies, who had snake hair, and the goddess Bona Dea, in whose temple live snakes were kept. In Norse mythology, you will come across the Midgard serpent, a giant snake that encircles the world. On and on it goes. Snakes pop up everywhere.

One of the most interesting archeological finds is a statue of a mother goddess and a child, both with snake heads. When I read about this discovery, I could not help but wonder why vipers were coupled with motherhood. After all, motherhood is usually honored with symbols of good, not evil. Then I remembered that in both Greek and Roman mythology there was a god named Aesculapius, known for his compassion and healing, two qualities caring mothers have. This god was typically pictured carrying a snake-entwined rod. The image is still with us today.

THE SNAKE ASSOCIATED WITH GOOD?

We have all seen it. Whenever a medical report is about to be presented on television, it is usually heralded by a caduceus, the symbol of the American Medical Association. A caduceus, as you may know, is an artist's representation of two snakes wrapped around a pole, often with wings at the top. At least that is one representation. The symbol can also be represented by a single snake on a tree branch—an image that reminds us of a mass healing that took place in Bible times. But how did civilization's primary symbol of evil get turned into a symbol of good? When and where did the switch occur?

I cannot account for the switch in other cultures, but I can account for it in the Judeo-Christian scheme of things. It all started when God's people, the Israelites, were on their way from Egypt to the Promised Land. Typically, these rebellious wanderers were disobeying God in almost everything He told them to do. God covered their sins with His mercy for a time. Then, seeing no change, He moved in righteous indignation. At one point, He sent poisonous snakes among His people (see Numbers 21:4–9). The reptiles God selected were of the *"fiery"* variety, we are told (KJV). This means that when they released their deadly venom, violent pain, accompanied by scarlet skin inflammation, raced up the victims' legs to their hearts. Some commentators tell of a red glow that appeared on the victims' faces as they were expiring. At any rate, these snakes caused deaths that were horrible, the Bible says.

Did this punishment accomplish what God intended? It did. The wayward masses came to a renewed sense of sin. They suddenly realized how deeply they had offended their holy God. But, as Bible commentator Matthew Henry observes, "[T]hey would not have owned the sin if they had not felt the smart."[9] In this regard, the Israelites typify all of us. We too are doomed to die unless—and it is a big *unless*—someone points out our problem, we accept the diagnosis and we willingly take advantage of the cure that is being offered.

In the case of the Israelites, Moses interceded on behalf of those who had been bitten, and God provided an antidote. The antidote, though, must have raised an eyebrow or two, for it was unusual. *"Make a snake and put it on a pole,"* God instructed Moses; *"anyone who is bitten can look on it and live"* (v 8).

"Make a *snake?*" Moses must have thought. "Snakes are *evil!* Snakes are causing people to die! Lord, You're telling me to make a *snake* and the snake will act as a cure!"

Yes, Moses, you have it right. A snake has caused your people's affliction, and a snake will provide their healing. (This is the point at which, in my opinion at least, the dreaded serpent went from being a symbol of evil to being a symbol of good. And Moses was among the first to observe the switch.)

How much significance the Israelites were able to attach to what happened there in the desert several hundred years before Christ is questionable. After all, those living before the cross saw through a glass *"darkly."* But we who are living on *this* side of the cross have God's Word to enlighten and to enrich us. The apostle John does just that when he writes, *"Just as Moses lifted up the snake in the desert, so the Son of Man must be lifted up, that everyone who believes in him may have eternal life"* (John 3:14).

From the above verse we deduce that the "pole" upon which the snake was fastened represented the future cross of Calvary, and the snake pointed to the Savior, who bore men's sins as He hung upon that cross. As the Scripture says, *"God made him who had no sin to be sin for us, so that in him we might become the righteousness of God"* (2 Corinthians

5:21). What? Did Jesus Christ have to become a "snake" in order to rid the world of "snakes"? you ask. Yes. He had to become sin in order to do away with it. This He did willingly. And He did it for you and for me.

But there is more to the symbolism before us. The snake in the desert, you will recall, was made of bronze. This means it was fashioned through a firing process. Our Savior went through flames, too, you will remember, the very flames of hell, as He bore His Father's wrath. It was wrath *our* sins, not His, deserved, for He was sinless. But He is the One who bore that wrath. And He bore it so that we might receive God's love.

In order to be cured of snakebite, an Israelite had to look to the snake on the pole. Then he would live. A sinner today has to look to the Christ on the cross. He has to face his own sinfulness, recognize his need for a cure, and want that cure desperately. Then he, too, will live. The look of faith is essential, no matter on which side of the cross one lives. For *"without faith it is impossible to please God,"* the Bible says (Hebrews 11:6).

Danger!

In our brief study of different cultures, we have seen how dangerous it is to make symbols out of snakes. The symbols can take on lives of their own, demanding allegiance.

"Look to me! Worship me! Serve me!" the bronze snake whispered to the unsuspecting Israelites in the desert; "Forget about the God I represent." Unfortunately, the Israelites allowed themselves to be seduced by this cry. They turned their symbol of healing into a pagan idol. Then they bowed down to it.

How long it took them to become so ensnared we do not know. What we *do* know is that by the time king Hezekiah came on the scene, worship of this bronze snake—the one the people had carried with them into the Promised Land—was routine. The new monarch knew he had to do something about this sacrilege. So he *"broke into pieces the bronze snake,"* the Bible says. Then we read, *"for up to that time the Israelites had been burning incense to it."* The snake even had a name. *"(It was called Nehushtan),"* we read (2 Kings 18:4).

Is there a lesson for us in the Israelites' entrapment? I believe so. The writer of Hebrews puts it well. *"Let us fix our eyes on Jesus, the author and finisher of our faith,"* he advises (12:2). In other words, let us focus on Christ our Savior and on Him alone! Let us do so with all our heart, our soul, and our strength. Let us be careful not to shift our focus to representations of Christ's atoning sacrifice—to things like ornamental crosses of silver and gold, which are only symbols. What Christ did on the cross is *real!* So let us look to *Him!* Honor *Him.* Worship *Him!*

Also, the next time we see a caduceus, medicine's symbol of hope, let us remember its spiritual significance. It points people to the One who can heal not only the body but the soul as well. As the prophet Isaiah aptly put it, *"the punishment that brought us peace was upon him (the Messiah), and by his wounds we are healed"* (Isaiah 53:5).

In summary, Christ on the cross bore evil's fiery curse in order to rid us of it. In God's complex plan of redemption, however, we know that permanent riddance of evil is a future, not a present, hope. Those of us living in the here and now are stuck with having to deal with the problems that evil is presently causing. What are we to do? Is there victory over sin in the routine of our everyday lives? Is there hope when temptation gets unbearable? Keep on reading. What lies ahead could be life-changing.

PART THREE

LESSONS TO LEARN: HOW TO HAVE VICTORY OVER SIN, SATAN AND TEMPTATION

"These things happened to them as examples and were written down as warnings for us, on whom the fulfillment of the ages has come. So if you think you are standing firm, be careful that you don't fall."

—1 Corinthians 10:11,12

Chapter 13

RECOGNIZE SATAN FOR WHO HE IS

"Woe to those who call evil good and good evil."
—Isaiah 5:20

E vil exists. We know that. We have pondered its origins and noted its pervasiveness. Yet the sovereign Lord reigns. We know that, too. We have marveled at how He can take something so detestable as sin and use it for purposes that are good. Yet He does. The cross of Jesus Christ is a good example of this phenomenon.

Now in this last section of our study, we want to examine sin more closely. How can we who are Christians resist the urge to do wrong? How can we keep from getting caught in Satan's snares?

HERE COMES TEMPTATION!

When the devil arrives on a Christian's front porch, he does not come wearing a name tag. He does not say, "Hello! My name is Satan. I am evil. I represent the powers of darkness and despair. I am here to do you harm. I intend to mess up your life, confuse your thinking, compromise your morals, reverse your priorities, harden your heart, deaden your conscience, blind you to truth, plug your ears, make you too busy to pray, tighten your lips when it comes to sharing your faith, and bind you so securely in self-centered pursuits that you don't have time to reach out to others."

Why, you would dismiss the stranger immediately. Satan knows this. So he comes in disguise, appearing as an *"angel of light"* (2 Corinthians 11:14). He presents himself as a mentor—someone who wants to help you in ways your God never could.

He usually begins by trying to discern how grounded his subject is in spiritual matters. It is the same technique he used on Eve in the Garden. "Did God really say what you think He said?" Satan will ask, planting doubts in your mind. "There are many interpretations of Scripture, you know. Accept whichever one you like best."

SLAM THAT DOOR!

You have just listened to a pack of lies! Satan is not trying to help you; he is out to destroy you! The Bible puts it this way: The devil *"leads the whole world astray"* (Revelation 12:9). He blinds those who do not know Christ

(2 Corinthians 4:4), and he wages warfare with those who *do* (Ephesians 6:11). He causes confusion and division (Matthew 13:25), steals sheep, kills dreams, and does anything else he can think of to destroy what honors the sovereign Lord (John 10:10). In short, Satan works at keeping unbelievers out of God's kingdom and rendering those already *in* God's kingdom ineffectual in their Christian service.

To accomplish his mission, Satan works subtly. For example, when it comes to the church, he introduces concepts that at first sound good but in the long run prove to be disastrous—concepts like tolerance, relativism, and syncretism. Any one of these concepts, if nurtured singly, can stifle the Holy Spirit's work. When all three are combined, they can split a congregation apart.

Take tolerance. "There is good in all religions," Satan whispers, "so don't correct somebody who proposes an unorthodox teaching in your Bible class. Rather, find something good to say about the remark and encourage open-minded discussion."

Consider relativism. "When it comes to morality," Satan continues, "realize you live in a post-modern world. You can not judge people by your own outdated morals. Step into the twenty-first century, my friend. Learn how to live in a world that is changing."

Then there is syncretism. "You're having trouble with some forms of contemporary worship, aren't you?" Satan taunts. "You are upset with the mixing of the sacred with the secular. How are you going to reach the world with the gospel if you don't bring the world into the sanctuary?"

To some Christians Satan's advice may sound plausible. After all, it is scriptural to keep *"the unity of the Spirit through the bond of peace"* (Ephesians 4:3). But what a ruse! Satan has just presented himself as a peacemaker, not the troublemaker that he is. As seventeenth-century Englishman Richard Greeham said, "It is the policy of the devil to persuade us that there is no devil."[10] The question is, will we let him?

Beware Of the Occult!

It behooves us to be especially wary when tempted to get involved in the occult. "Really now," Satan whispers, trying to sound rational, "what's wrong with a little experimentation now and then with a ouija board—or with having your palm read—or your fortune told? What's wrong with consulting an astrologer, participating in a little witchcraft, or going to an evening séance? These things can be enlightening, stimulating, *fun!"*

The Bible warns against such practices. *"Let no one be found among you who...practices divination or sorcery, interprets omens, engages in witchcraft or casts spells, or who is a medium or spiritist or who consults the dead,"* it says. *"Anyone who does these things is detestable to the Lord..."* (Deuteronomy 18:10–12).

Detestable or not, Satan encourages us to dive in. Believe it or not, he has made dabbling in the occult a popular, even a socially-acceptable thing to do. He has accomplished this feat through popular authors who write about demons and spells, movie and television producers who feature dark themes in their shows, and newspaper editors who give precious space to astrologers. Even séances pass the raised eyebrow test today. In fact, many grieving widows and widowers are told that attending a séance is a "must" if they want to get over their mourning.

Generally speaking, mediums conducting séances do not have the power to summon spirits of the dead. What they *can* summon, however, are spirits "familiar" with the spirits of the dead—spirits who fool grieving loved ones into thinking they are encountering the real thing. Although many mediums are downright fakes, there are indeed some who have made an actual connection to the world of evil spirits, including the world of "familiar spirits."

The witch of Endor in the Bible was one of the latter kind. She was accustomed to calling up deceased loved ones and watching a "familiar spirit" take the dead one's place. One day, however, a frightening thing happened. The dead person she called up actually appeared. It was the prophet Samuel, miraculously delivered by the Lord to rebuke king Saul for his sin. When the witch saw Samuel rising up out of the ground, she was so traumatized *"she cried out at the top of her voice,"* the Bible says (1 Samuel 28:12). What can we Christians learn from this encounter? Just this: you never know what is going to happen in a séance—or with a ouija board—or with the casting of a spell. So it is wise to stay away from anything and everything that smacks of the occult.

Another caution: realize that not only have some demonic spirits become familiar with certain individuals and *their* ways but some have also become familiar with the Lord and *His* ways. When Jesus was speaking at a synagogue in Capernaum, he was interrupted by a man *"possessed by an evil spirit,"* the Bible says. The man cried out, *"What do you want with us, Jesus of Nazareth? Have you come to destroy us? I know who you are—the Holy One of God"* (Mark 1:24).

The fact that these demons have become familiar with the Lord poses a danger to Christians who have opened themselves to occult practices. It means these demons can make these Christians think they are getting messages from the heavenly Father when, in fact, they are listening to wily impersonators—impersonators who are good at feigning the Lord's voice. That is why every notion, thought, concept, or idea has to be measured against what God has said in His Word. The Bible is the only message we have that is infallible, inerrant, authoritative, and totally trustworthy.

TEST THE SPIRITS!

When it comes to discerning between the true and the false, the Lord comes to our aid. What follows are some questions we can ask ourselves whenever we are in doubt about a message we have just heard or a religious practice we have just witnessed. To make the questions personal, fill in the blanks with the name of the person you are wondering about.

1. Does _____ preach the word of God and only the Word of God? Is the Word usually preached in context? Is the Word ever twisted to fit a personal agenda? In order for God to approve a message or a religious practice, it must square with biblical truth. So use your Bible as your

standard, holding everything you hear and see up to it. It is a *"more sure word of prophecy,"* the apostle Peter says, your ultimate yardstick for discernment (2 Peter 1:19 KJV).

Beware of those who reference the Bible in their sermons, yet add to what it says. Understand that the Lord is not giving new revelation. So, if a preacher claims to have a special "word from the Lord," be suspicious. God says He has already given us everything we need for faith and practice (2 Peter 1:3). Nothing more is necessary for our spiritual well-being.

Be equally suspicious of those who take away from God's Word. When Satan tempted Jesus in the wilderness (See Matthew 4:1–11), he omitted portions of the texts he was quoting. By doing so he could give certain passages the thrust that he wanted. This technique is as old as history itself, and is still being used by the devil today.

2. **Am I attracted to _____ 's ministry because the Lord is exalted through it or because I see "miracles" being performed? Do _____ 's messages and miracles draw me closer to God or push me away from God?** In Old Testament times a prophet who misled God's people was charged with a capital crime. Listen to what Moses said to the people he was leading through the wilderness: *"If a prophet or one who foretells by dreams appears among you and announces to you a miraculous sign or wonder and if the sign or wonder of which he has spoken takes place, and he says 'Let us follow other gods' (gods you have not known) 'and let us worship them,' you must not listen to the words of that prophet or dreamer....That prophet or dreamer must be put to death...; he has tried to turn you from the way the Lord*

your God has commanded you to follow. You must purge the evil from among you" (Deuteronomy 13:1,5).

3. **Does _____ predict the future? If so, does every prediction come true?** Prophets who are sent from the Lord do not make mistakes. They are 100 percent correct every time. When the Israelites asked, "*How can we know when a message has not been spoken by the Lord?*" the answer was, "*If what a prophet proclaims in the name of the Lord does not take place or come true, that is a message the Lord has not spoken. That prophet has spoken presumptuously. Do not be afraid of him*" (Deuteronomy 18:21,22).

4. **Does _____ lead a God-glorifying life?** The Bible warns, "*Watch out for false prophets. They come to you in sheep's clothing, but inwardly they are ferocious wolves. By their fruit you will recognize them…*" (Matthew 7:15,16). In his letter to the Galatians, the apostle Paul contrasts "*acts of a sinful nature*" with the "*fruit of the Spirit.*" Whereas the one is characterized by "*sexual immorality, impurity and debauchery; idolatry and witchcraft; hatred, discord, jealousy, fits of rage, selfish ambition, dissensions, factions and envy; drunkenness, orgies, and the like,*" the other is marked by "*love, joy, peace, patience, kindness, goodness, faithfulness, gentleness, and self-control*" (Galatians 5:19–21). What a contrast!

5. **What do respected Christian leaders think of _____ and of his/her ministry?** "*Every matter must be established by the testimony of two or three witnesses,*" the Bible says (2 Corinthians 13:1). "*Listen to advice and accept instruction, and in the end you will be wise*" (Proverbs 19:20). "*The spirits of prophets are subject to the control of prophets.*

For God is not a God of disorder but of peace" (1 Corinthians 14:32,33). With these admonitions in mind, consult with leaders you admire to see what *they* have to say about the one who is influencing you. If you get negative feedback, you may be sitting under a counterfeit teacher.

6. **Is it possible that a false spirit may be at work in the life and ministry of _____?** To find out, ask a question revealed in God's Word. If the "prophet" has difficulty forming the answer, be wary. *"Dear friends,"* the apostle John says, *"do not believe every spirit, but test the spirits to see if they are from God, because many prophets have gone out into the world. This is how you can recognize the Spirit of God: Every spirit that acknowledges that Jesus Christ has come in the flesh is from God, but every spirit that does not acknowledge Jesus is not from God. This is the spirit of antichrist, which you have heard is coming and even now is already in the world"* (1 John 4:1–3).

There you have it: several tests suggested by the Lord for discerning what is true and what is false. These are tests we Christians need; for when Satan comes knocking on the door, he does not come wearing a name tag. But he does come wearing a smile. That is why discernment is necessary. Planning ahead for possible Satanic attacks also helps.

Chapter 14

TAKE PRECAUTIONS TO AVOID EVIL AND ALL APPEARANCES OF IT

"Test everything. Hold on to the good. Avoid every kind of evil."

—1 Thessalonians 5:22

What happens when people fail to plan ahead of time to protect themselves from sin's consequences? Consider the following scenarios:

1. A pastor visits a porn site on his computer. Before long he is "hooked." For a while he is able to keep his addiction from his family and his congregation. Then one day someone finds out and broadcasts his discovery. Although the pastor admits his transgression and asks for forgiveness, the damage has been done. His wife files for divorce, and his church votes to expel him. It is a sad time for all—all except for the local newspaper editor, who seizes the opportunity to print a sure-to-sell story of moral depravity.

2. A Sunday school teacher of pre-teens is seen coming out of an establishment known for its "stimulating adult entertainment." When confronted, the teacher explains that he was "witnessing to sinners." When word about the incident spreads, his class members are devastated. They wonder how they are going to explain their teacher's behavior to their friends at school. They also discuss whether they can ever trust a Christian role model again.

3. Two recent graduates of a church youth group decide to take a trip to Europe together. Both are known to have taken "abstinence vows." Nevertheless, tongues wag. Why would Christian young people participate in an activity that gives the impression of being evil even if it is not? Why would their Christian parents let them? Gossip continues long after the couple returns, virginity reportedly intact.

The above scenarios speak volumes about the power of evil, even the power of apparent evil, to destroy lives. Although each situation is different, the results are surprisingly similar. Reputations are damaged, friends and family members are hurt, the testimony of the church is compromised, and the world is throwing up its hands and proclaiming, "See! I told you so. Those Christians are no different from the rest of us!"

Are these the kinds of results we want our faith in Christ to produce? If not, what can we do to keep our testimonies pure? The answer, according to Scripture, is avoidance—avoidance not only of obvious, overt sin, but also of any "*appearance*" of sin (1 Thessalonians 5:22 KJV). To help us achieve this goal, the Bible cautions us to monitor what we look at, to be careful where we go and who goes with us, and to watch what we do, considering how our actions might be interpreted by others.

MONITORING WHAT WE LOOK AT

According to the Bible, our eyes are the lamps of our bodies. Jesus told his disciples, *"When your eyes are good, your whole body is full of light. But when they are bad, your body also is full of darkness"* (Luke 11:34). The patriarch Job must have been aware of this danger; for even though he lived before his Redeemer articulated it, he claimed, *"I made a covenant with my eyes not to look lustfully at a girl"* (Job 31:1).

It is too bad king David did not make such a covenant; for it was his eyes, you will remember, that got him into trouble with Bathsheba. Adam's wife Eve should have made such a covenant too. The Bible implies that when she gazed upon the forbidden fruit—fruit which was *"pleasing to the eye"* (Genesis 3:6)—her act of sinning was as good as done. Right then!

Ham, the son of Noah, also succumbed to the temptation of the eyes. He looked upon the nakedness of his father, the Scripture says, and was cursed because of it (see Genesis 9:20–25). Then there was Lot's wife, who *"looked back"* when she was fleeing the destruction of Sodom and Gomorrah and was turned into a *"pillar of salt"* (Genesis 19:26). Yet another casualty was Esau, who saw the meat his brother Jacob was preparing for his father and craved it so much he gave up his birthright in exchange for it (see Genesis 25:30). It is amazing the power the eyes have on the action the body takes, is it not?

There are many more examples of "eye problems" in the Bible. I will name but a few. When Shechem *"saw"* Dinah, the daughter of Jacob, *"he took her and violated her,"* the Scriptures say (Genesis 34:2). After a victorious battle, Achan, a participant, told Joshua, *"When I saw in the plunder a beautiful robe from Babylonia, two hundred shekels of silver and a wedge of gold weighing fifty shekels, I coveted them and took them"* (Joshua 7:21). When Samson, the Bible character known for his strength, was still young, he told his parents, *"I have seen a Philistine woman in Timnah; now get her to me as my wife"* (Judges 14:2). Later, *"he saw a prostitute in Gaza, and went in to spend the night with her"* (Judges 16:1). Still later, he allowed himself to be lured by Delilah, who nagged him relentlessly until he told her that the secret of his strength was his hair. Having learned this, she turned him over to the Philistines who shaved his head, bound him with shackles, and mercilessly gouged out his eyes. What an ironic twist to the life of a man who had taken a vow to serve the Lord with his body, yet could not control a small part of that body.

King Solomon also needed a spiritual ophthalmologist. Although he wrote proverbs that reflected wisdom, he fell short of his own advice. In warning against sexual sin, he wrote, *"Do not lust in your heart after* [an adulteress'] *beauty or let her captivate you with her eyes"* (Proverbs 6:25), yet in his own life he allowed many women to do just that. It was a sin for which he would pay dearly. We are told that in

Solomon's later years, *"his wives turned his heart after other gods....He followed Ashtoreth, the goddess of the Sidonians, and Molech, the detestable god of the Ammonites. So Solomon did evil in the eyes of the Lord..."* (1 Kings 11:4–6).

I wonder: Are we any wiser today? The culture in which we are living presents a multitude of temptations, many of which are geared to seduce us through our eyes. There are over two million porn sites on the Internet worldwide, we are told, to say nothing of the number of sexually explicit movies, videos, and TV shows that can be beamed right into our living rooms, dens, and bedrooms. In addition, there are a host of sleazy books and tabloids prominently displayed in our local stores and an endless barrage of provocative billboards that assault our eye gates every day. Put all these images together, and you have some idea of how effective Satan's marketing strategy is. You can also see from Satan's success with the pastor in scenario #1 how vulnerable we are if we do not plan to protect ourselves in advance.

Perhaps, if we have never done it before, now is the time to follow Job's example and make a covenant with our eyes. This means vowing not to watch, read, or dwell upon things that are evil but, rather, to dwell upon things that are *"true, noble, right, pure, lovely, admirable, excellent, or praiseworthy"* (see Philippians 4:8). Then when tempted, we will be in a better position to resist. Jesus resisted, you will remember, when Satan *"showed Him all the kingdoms of the world and their splendor"* and promised to give them all to Him if He would simply bow His knee (Matthew 4:8,9).

I know what you are saying: "But I'm not Jesus! I'm human! I'm weak!" This is true. But the same Spirit who was living in Jesus Christ now lives in us. And that Spirit has the same power over sin today that He had back then. *"Turn my eyes away from worthless things,"* we can pray; *"Open my eyes that I may see wonderful things in your law"* (Psalms 119:37,18). Then we listen to that still, small voice within. It says, "Click off that porn site, Christian! Switch to another channel! Toss that trashy novel into the waste basket! Start reading your Bible!" These are just some of the tips God gives us for stopping evil in its tracks and doing so at the vulnerable eye-gate.

BEING CAREFUL WHERE WE GO AND WHO GOES WITH US

The Bible tell us that godliness requires controlling our feet as well as our eyes. It involves learning to say no when tempted to go somewhere we know we should not go. The Sunday school teacher in scenario # 2 should have known better. Places that offer adult entertainment are not places for a Christian to be. Even if the teacher were in the establishment for the purpose of witnessing to sinners (as he claimed to be), his influence as a role model should have signaled, "Do not go there!"

The teenagers who traveled together in scenario # 3 should have known better as well. They did something that created the impression of being wrong even if no wrong was done. The Scriptures say, *"But among you there must not be even a hint of sexual immorality or any kind of impurity"* (Ephesians 5:3).

I myself learned about avoiding the appearance of evil the hard way. Shortly after becoming a Christian, I was asked to serve on a committee at church. It met at night. Named to the same committee was a gentleman who lived close by. Because I did not like driving in the dark I asked my friend if he would mind picking me up. To my surprise, he said he could not do that.

Then he explained why. "Both of us are happily married," he said, "but we are not married to each other. I am a retired minister with a reputation to preserve, and you are a young believer with a reputation to build upon. Suppose we had a car accident. Can you imagine the story the local paper would print: 'Last evening the Reverend So-and-So was driving to church with a certain Mrs. Rankin when they were rammed by a vehicle traveling west on Route 62'—or some such thing. How would that look?"

I swallowed hard, thanked my friend for his wisdom, and proceeded to drive myself to the meetings. It has been years since that incident happened, but I am still conscious of the fact that I should think twice about getting into a car alone with a member of the opposite sex, other than my husband, that is.

A biblical nugget reads as follows: *"He who walks with the wise grows wise, but a companion of fools suffers harm"* (Proverbs 13:20). In other words, it is important to choose friends who will be a good influence—friends who will seek to preserve not only their own reputations, but ours as well—friends who will take seriously the following Scriptures: 1) *"Make level paths for your feet and take only ways that are firm. Do not swerve to the right or to*

the left; keep your foot from evil" (Proverbs 4:26,27) and
2) "Do not set your foot on the path of the wicked or walk in
the way of evil men. Avoid it, do not travel on it; turn from
it and go your way" (Proverbs 4:14,15). I am glad I had a
friend who was aware of the wisdom tucked away in these
verses, even though I myself was not. He helped me keep
my testimony for the Lord Jesus Christ pure.

Watching What We Do, Realizing How It Might Be Interpreted

Young people are especially vulnerable to falling into
"appearances" of evil, it seems, even when the intents of
their hearts are proper. How can we adults prepare them to
make wise biblical decisions? My husband and I ask ourselves this question every time we do a seminar for youth.
We have come up with a technique designed not only to
protect them personally but to protect their testimonies as
well. It involves drawing a cross. This cross will remind
them not only of Jesus' sacrifice on their behalf, we explain,
but also of their responsibilities to the various individuals
in their lives. The top part of the cross, we demonstrate,
points toward God; the bottom, toward themselves; the
right arm, to their fellow Christian friends; and the left arm,
to their non-Christian friends. We suggest four questions
to ask themselves as they weigh the consequences of their
decisions:

1. **Will what I am about to do bring glory, honor, and
   praise to the Lord Jesus Christ?** The Bible says,

"So whether you eat or drink or whatever you do, do it all for the glory of God" (1 Corinthians 10:31). Since glorifying God is the primary reason for our existence, this is the first and foremost question to ask. If the answer is no, there may be no need to ask any other questions. If, however, the answer is not definitive ("Well, what I am planning to do may not bring glorify to God, but it won't take away from His glory either"), then it is time to ask question number two.

2. **Will participating in this activity make me a better person?** The apostle Paul warns, *"Everything is permissible—but not everything is beneficial. Everything is permissible—but not everything is constructive"* (1 Corinthians 10:23). Since God is in the process of making vessels of honor for His name's sake, this question is an important one. Unfortunately, many Christians do things they know will harm them—why, I am not sure.

   Our oldest son, Dirk, thankfully, learned how to make wise decisions early. One day, after he had become an adult, his father asked him what had kept him from succumbing to some of the temptations that had ensnared many of his high school companions. "I weighed the consequences of my actions ahead of time," Dirk answered. "I figured it was either 'pay now or pay later.' I guess I felt that losing a few friends in high school was better than losing more important things later on." My husband, Lee, smiled. So did I when I learned of the revealing conversation. Dirk is now passing this wisdom on to his own children, trusting God for their protection as well. Thank you, Lord!

3. **If my Christian friends find out I did this, could it cause them to stumble in their walk with Christ?** The apostle Paul took this matter seriously, coming to the following conclusion: *"Therefore if what I eat causes my brother to fall into sin, I will never eat meat again, so that I will not cause him to fall"* (1 Corinthians 8:13). How sensitive the apostle was to the damage his actions could do to those looking up to him! Can we modern-day Christians be any less sensitive to those looking up to *us*?

4. **If my non-Christian friends find out I have done this, will it hinder my attempts to reach them with the gospel?** Again the apostle comes to a conclusion. Essentially he decides, "I will do nothing that others may interpret as a breach of God's law, even though the action itself passes my own standard of behavior." He gives his reason: *"I am not seeking my own good, but the good of many that they may be saved"* (1 Corinthians 10:33). What passion the apostle had for winning the lost!

A SUMMARY

In his letter to the Romans, the apostle shares the basis for the whole of his decision-making process, including all four arms of our "cross." *"For none of us lives to himself alone,"* he says, *"and none of us dies to himself alone. If we live, we live to the Lord; and if we die, we die to the Lord"* (Romans 14:7,8). He could have added, "We also belong to each other," for the body of Christ is a community. So is the world in general. Every action an individual takes affects someone for good or for ill. Therefore, it behooves us to watch very carefully what we do and how we do it.

No matter how many precautions we Christians may take to avoid sinning, however, there will be times when suddenly temptation is standing right in front of us, beckoning. When this happens, there may be only one action to take: flee. For a contemporary example of someone who did just that, read on.

Chapter 15

WHEN TEMPTED TO SIN, RUN!

"Flee from sexual immorality."

—1 Corinthians 6:18

G et moving! Leave the scene! Go! In other words, when running away from evil is an option, take it.

I am going to turn the beginning of this chapter over to my husband Lee, who is now retired, but who spent many years in the business world. I want him to tell you, in his own words, about a temptation he faced in the marketplace and about how God provided *"a way to escape"* and he took it. Here's Lee:

"There I was—a Christian businessman, a dedicated family man, a church elder, and a Sunday school teacher—standing in front of a strip joint, being threatened with the loss of a large order if I didn't go inside. How did I get myself in such a predicament? It was easy.

"I was, at the time this incident took place, the Detroit District Sales Manager for Siemens Medical Systems, the world's largest supplier of medical equipment. Siemens, a German company, manufacturers a variety of systems, including CT and MRI scanners, heart catherization units, ultrasound units, and radiation therapy systems. I was escorting several radiologists from a teaching hospital in Detroit to our factory outside Nuremberg. This trip was important to me because I needed the business for my district, and I needed the commission for myself. (We would soon have three sons in college at the same time.) The hospital administration was talking about purchasing up to three CT scanners. That order would meet both financial needs nicely.

"The trip occurred at a time when CT technology was being introduced to the United States market, and the Siemens scanner offered several state-of-the-art features that were not available on competitive units. I was hoping our technological advances would convince the doctors to buy from me. If they did, their order would place the first Siemens CT scanner in Michigan. Not only that, it would place the first Siemens scanner in the whole Midwest. So I didn't have to think twice about having the Detroit office pick up the tab for the trip.

IN GERMANY

"The factory visit went extremely well—so well that the order looked, as I would say today, like a "slam dunk." The second part of the trip, the visit to a local hospital to observe patient scanning, also went well. To my delight, the image quality of the scanner was superb, and the speed of the system was impressive. My customers were giving me signals that they were interested in buying from me. "This system will give our hospital the competitive edge we need," they said. When I heard that remark, I felt good. But I kept reminding myself that nothing is in the bag until the signed purchase order is in the hand. I had learned this from previous experiences.

"There was one more event to attend before we left for home the next morning. That was a farewell banquet planned by our factory hosts. As you may know, Germans enjoy long, lingering meals, consisting of several courses. This one would be no exception. For a special treat, our hosts had selected a small restaurant in the fabled walled city of Nuremberg. They told us that during the war years, the previous owner of the restaurant had buried all the establishment's valuables outside the city so they would not be damaged. Now those valuables were back in place, adding to the history as well as to the ambience of the place.

"The doctors and I enjoyed every minute of our time at the restaurant. When the dinner was over, we went outside to hail taxis. Once we saw what a beautiful evening it was and we realized that our hotel was only a dozen blocks away, we decided to walk instead. As we negotiated the uneven cobblestone streets, everyone seemed to be in a good mood. Then we turned a corner. There it was: the strip joint. Right in front of us!

"As we were approaching the entrance, the head physician and primary decision-maker stopped and turned toward the group. 'Let's go in,' he announced, a sense of adventure in his voice. I was shocked. But I managed to reply as politely as possible that anybody who wanted to go in was free to do so but that I would not be going in with them.

"'Sure you will,' the doctor said. Then he told me not to worry because 'Your wife will never know.'

"I told him my wife most certainly *would* know. She would see it in my eyes. I then repeated my resolve to keep walking. 'This club is not part of my factory tour,' I emphasized.

"Everybody laughed at that remark. But the primary decision maker continued to pressure me. I could see from the determination on his face that he was not going to take no for an answer. I must say, however, that I was not prepared for what happened next. He turned, looked me squarely in the eye and threatened, 'If you don't go inside, you will not get our order.'

"I was stunned. I could not believe the doctor's lack of professionalism. But, by the grace of God, I was ready for it. I stared him back and said, 'If that's what it takes to get your business, I guess I don't need your business. Good evening, gentlemen. I'll see you in the lobby for breakfast at 8 AM.' Then I walked away, leaving my companions standing in front of the club.

"It was then that my heart started pounding. I thought it was going to leap right out of my chest. Here comes 'the big one!' I thought. Then I started to weep. In all probability I had just lost a large commission. But that was not the reason for my tears. I was so grateful to God I had not caved in and denied Him that my emotions just overflowed. I couldn't get over the moral strength that was there when I had needed it most.

"The next morning our group met in the hotel lobby for breakfast as planned. Everyone was cordial. No one said a word about the street scene, and I was not about to bring it up. However, when one of the physicians got me alone, he asked if I thought less of him for what he had done the night before. I told him that I had provided a real banquet for him, with all the trimmings, but that for dessert he had chosen to eat 'garbage.' His choice to enter the strip joint had disappointed me.

BACK HOME

"We arrived back in Michigan without incident. The minute I opened the front door, Peg was there. 'How did it go?' she asked. 'Do you think you'll get their business?' I told her the order was in jeopardy. Would it come through after all? I really didn't know.

"Later on I shared with our whole family the details of what had happened. As I described the scene on the sidewalk in front of the strip club, our sons' eyes got as big as saucers. 'You never know when you will come face to face with temptation,' I said. 'You have to be ready all the time.' As I was speaking these words, however, I was aware of my own frailties, of what could have happened. And I was wondering about our family's future. Would God influence the hearts of the physicians to give me the order? Or would He provide for us in some other way altogether?

"It was about two weeks after the trip ended that I received a phone call from the hospital's purchasing department. The voice on the other end of the line told me to come down and pick up my order. It would not be for the three CT scanners I was hoping for, I learned; but it would be for two. That was more than enough.

"When I got off the phone, I let out a loud *Y-e-e-s-s!* God had come through for me again. He didn't have to, but He had. I called Peg with the news. Then I got alone with my Lord so I could thank Him for His amazing grace. *'Rejoice in the Lord always,'* He reminded me as I opened my Bible. *'I will say it again: Rejoice!...Do not be anxious about anything, but in everything, by prayer and petition, with thanksgiving, present your requests to God. And the peace of God, which transcends all understanding, will guard your hearts and your minds in Christ Jesus....And my God will meet all your needs according to his glorious riches in Christ Jesus'* (Philippians 4:4,6–7,19). These words are among my favorites, even to this day; for they remind me of what faithfulness is all about. It's not about me at all. It's all about Him—my loving, compassionate Lord—a Lord who never, never fails!"

THINGS TO REMEMBER
WHEN SIN BECKONS

1. **God is watching me, even if nobody else is.** We tend to think that we can relax our morals a bit when we are alone—or if we are with people we will never see again—or if we are in a place that is far from home. Nobody will notice, we think. Nobody will

know what we are about. And nobody will care if we fall. But we are wrong. God notices, God cares, and God holds us accountable for the choices we make. The Bible puts it this way: *"Nothing in all creation is hidden from God's sight. Everything is uncovered and laid bare before the eyes of him to whom we must give account"* (Hebrews 4:13).

The thought of God's omniscience made king David uncomfortable. In psalm 139 he exclaimed, *"O Lord, you have searched me and you know me. You know when I sit and when I rise; you perceive my thoughts from afar. You discern my going out and my lying down; you are familiar with all my ways."* Then he blurted out, *"Where can I go from your Spirit? Where can I flee from your presence? If I go to the heavens, you are there; if I make my bed in the depths, you are there."* (vv 1–3,7,8). In the next few verses, however, the king spends time contemplating the benefits of God's watch-care over him. This turns out to be a wise move, for by the end of the psalm, we hear him welcoming the Lord's scrutiny. *"Search me, O God,"* David cries, *"and know my heart; test me and know my anxious thoughts. See if there is any offensive way in me and lead me in the way everlasting"* (vv 23,24).

When it comes to temptation, it is a blessing that God sees all. He can spot "exits" we might not be aware of, and He can turn us toward them. He is the One who does the turning, but we are the ones who must do the "exiting." It is the responsibility of every Christian to *"flee sexual immorality,"* the Bible says (1 Corinthians 6:18). It is also our responsibility to flee any other temptation Satan might decide to send our way.

2. **Those close to me will sense it if I have failed to resist temptation.** My husband Lee was correct when he said I would know it if he gave in to Satan's wiles. I would. I would see it in his face. I would hear it in his voice. I would feel it in his touch. You cannot fool a marriage partner who knows you well—one with whom you have shared the most intimate moments of your life.

You can not fool your children either, not even the youngest ones. When you pick up your Bible to lead them in family devotions—or when you ask God to bless the food they are about to eat—or when you bend down to give them a goodnight kiss, they will sense a difference. Should they find out what brought about that difference (either through the gossip of friends, or through an age-appropriate confession on your part), they will wonder why you did not flee the scene. After all, the Joseph in their Bible story did.

Most children start out thinking the best of their elders. They do not anticipate the possibility that a trusted parent might be living a lie. Should they find out one has been, they feel betrayed. This feeling may take a long time to go away.

3. **My conscience will warn me of impending danger.** This is true. The conscience speaks up when its host is being threatened. Should that host give in to temptation's beckoning, the conscience will continue to speak out until the sin that has been committed is confessed to God. King David found this out. After he sinned with Bathsheba, his conscience made such a racket that it affected his whole body. He was not able

to recover, you will remember, until he articulated his sin to the Lord.

The apostle Paul, on the other hand, tells of a good experience with *his* conscience. In writing to the Corinthians, he identified with the behavior of his traveling companions and commended it. *"Our conscience testifies that we have conducted ourselves in the world, especially in our relations with you,"* he boasted gratefully, *"in the holiness and sincerity that are from God. We have done so not according to worldly wisdom but according to God's grace"* (2 Corinthians 1:12). In this case the conscience defended, rather than accused, the Lord's followers because they had listened to it (see Romans 2:15).

4. **Memorizing Scripture will give me strength when I need it.** The Word of God is the greatest spiritual protection there is. Since we do not always have access to our physical Bibles, it is important to hide God's Word in our hearts. What we have memorized will alert us to the degree of danger we are in and give us the courage to flee if necessary.

In summary, God has promised to provide a *"way out"* of tempting situations (1 Corinthians 10:13). One *"way out"* is verbal; the other, physical. Joseph tried using words with Potiphar's wife you will remember, before running out the door; and my husband Lee did the same with his physician friends before turning his back and proceeding up the German street. Whatever exit God provides, we want to be ready to go through it. We want to escape Satan's snares with our values and morality in tact.

We all know, however, that sometimes running away is not an option. Sometimes we have to stay and fight. To be reminded of the arsenal of spiritual weapons available to the Christian, continue reading.

Chapter 16

WHEN RUNNING IS NOT
AN OPTION, FIGHT!

*"Put on the full armor of God so that you can take your
stand against the devil's schemes."*

—Ephesians 6:11

Wise monarchs prepare for war. They stockpile ammunition in the event of attack. The sovereign Lord is no exception. He has an arsenal of weapons for fighting the powers of darkness. He expects His soldiers to use these weapons when His kingdom is threatened.

We Christians make up the Lord's "army." One of our assignments is to do battle in His name against *"the spiritual forces of evil"* (Ephesians 6:12). Since the war we are fighting is spiritual in nature, so are our weapons. According to the Bible, these weapons include a *"belt of truth,"* a *"breastplate of righteousness,"* shoes fitted to carry *"the gospel of peace,"* a *"shield of faith,"* a *"helmet of salvation,"* and a *"sword of the Spirit, which is the word of God."* As we go into battle, we are instructed to stay in contact with the One giving the orders, for prayer completes the weaponry we have been issued. Let us examine our "arms" one at a time.

THE BELT OF TRUTH

Ever since sin entered the world, humankind has been pursuing a false ideal. It is the same ideal that trapped Eve in the Garden. *"You [can] become like God,"* Satan told her, *"knowing good and evil"* (Genesis 3:5). She believed him. Unfortunately, everyone born since then has believed him too. Ask the apostle Paul. Fallen man has *"exchanged the truth of God for a lie,"* he says (Romans 1:25). It is the lie that an individual can run his own life better than God can run it for him. What folly!

To prove to the world how false this lie is, God the Father sent Truth to planet Earth in the Person of Jesus Christ. *"The reason the Son of God appeared,"* the Bible makes clear, *"was to destroy the devil's work"* (1 John 3:8). Listen to what Jesus said about His own mission: *"I am the way, the truth and the life....If you hold to my teachings, you are really my disciples. Then you will know the truth and truth will set you free"* (John 14:6 and 8:31). When Jesus left the earth to return to His Father, He sent the Holy Spirit, whom He called the *"Spirit of Truth,"* as His replacement. Now we believers have Someone living within us who promises not only to remind us of the truth we have been taught, but also to *"guide"* us into the remainder of God's truth (see John 16:13).

"Stand firm then," the Bible advises, *"with the belt of truth buckled around your waist"* (Ephesians 6:14). Whenever I read these words, I picture a heavy lifter slipping into his back support. When he tightens his belt, he can stand up straight, even when the load he is carrying is massive. The sovereign Lord has provided us with the ability to stand for righteousness, to avoid compromise, and to live in a way that not only honors God, but also respects our fellow travelers. We, however, have to "put on" the provision God has made for us and draw it tightly around us.

The Breastplate of Righteousness

A soldier's breastplate covers his heart, that vital organ which pumps life into his whole body. If the heart receives a blow, the rest of the body suffers. If the blow is severe enough, the body could die.

No wonder Satan targets the heart. If he can deliver a blow there, he will have delivered a blow everywhere. Knowing this, Satan aims carefully, choosing areas that are critical to the Christian's belief system—areas like trust in God, assurance of eternal life, and a sense of one's worth in Christ. "Your Lord really failed you this time, didn't He?" Satan will taunt. "How can you call yourself a Christian and do the things that you do? You're a real loser, my friend—a real loser."

Thankfully, Jesus Christ comes to our aid at times like these. When we are unfairly challenged or falsely accused, He rises as our attorney to defend us. *"Who will bring any charge against those whom God has chosen?"* He asks

(Romans 8:33). The answer? "No one." For as the Lord is defending us, He is holding His own breastplate over our hearts. When the Judge looks upon His Son's breastplate, He sees the Son's righteousness. "Not guilty" He declares. What welcome words these are to the redeemed sinner's ear!

Our imputed righteousness, however, does not release us Christians from forming our own value systems and faithfully living them out. Hopefully, we will have settled on what we believe and why we believe it before Satan inflicts too much damage on us. When God instructs us to make sure our breastplates of righteousness are *"in place"* (Ephesians 6:14), He is encouraging us to live our Christian beliefs so convincingly that Satan is deprived of areas to attack . *"[P]ut off your old self,"* the apostle Paul advises, *"which is being corrupted by evil desires,"* and *"[P]ut on the new self, created to be like God in righteousness and holiness"* (Ephesians 4:22,24). In other words, live up to your profession of faith. Strive to become the Christian soldier your "uniform" says you are! Make your Commander-in-chief proud.

SHOES FITTED TO CARRY THE GOSPEL OF PEACE

In Bible times, there was no postal system as we know it today. Instead, there were messengers who delivered personal messages and general news. If you lived in a society that disseminated information this way, you would learn quickly how to gauge the gait of the messenger coming toward you. If he was advancing hesitantly, dragging his feet, he was a bearer of bad news. If, on the other hand, the messenger was running swiftly, he was bringing news that was good.

This is why the Bible says, *"How beautiful are the feet of those who bring good news!"* (Romans 10:15). We messengers of the gospel are bringing not only good news but the best news of all! "Jesus Christ died to redeem sinners!" we proclaim. "Enemies of God can be reconciled to their Maker! Those who are living in turmoil can experience peace: peace with God, peace with each other, and peace within themselves!"

Satan does not like this news. "I must keep those people on planet Earth under my thumb," he resolves. "I must keep them at war with God, rebelling against anything and everything spiritual. I must keep them at each other's throats, causing one another heartache and pain. I must keep them churning and writhing within, in personal turmoil. These people are mine. I must never lose control over them. *Never!"*

But you will, Satan. You will—if Christians carry the gospel of peace.

The Shield of Faith

After a soldier dons the other parts of his armor, he picks up his trusted shield. Because of the shield's maneuverability, the soldier considers it an important part of his protective gear. He uses it to ward off blows headed toward areas the rest of his metal does not cover.

The Christian's *"shield"* is his faith. With faith he can *"extinguish the flaming arrows of the evil one,"* the Bible says

(Ephesians 6:16). One's shield of faith does not have to be large, we are told. In fact, it can be as small as a *"grain of mustard seed"* and still be effective (Matthew 17:20). It just has to cover the right spot at the right time.

Satan's "arrows" are dipped in different kinds of poison. One of these poisons is designed to create personal fears. In Jesus' day, there were some who believed the Man from Nazareth might be their Messiah, yet *"they would not confess their faith for fear they would be put out of the synagogue,"* the Bible says (John 12:42). If they had lifted their shields of faith, so to speak, they would have proved they were on the side of Christ. As it was, they proved the opposite—with sad results. *"Whoever acknowledges me before men,"* Jesus said, *"I will also acknowledge him before my Father in heaven. But whoever disowns me before men, I will disown before my Father in heaven"* (Matthew 10:32,33).

Other arrows of Satan raise personal doubts. Remember how the evil one attacked Eve in the Garden? *"Did God say…?"* he asked her, planting seeds of uncertainty in her mind. The Bible says, *"Now faith is being sure of what we hope for and certain of what we do not see"* (Hebrews 11:1, emphases added). Faith is the weapon we have been given to fight the doubts Satan plants in our minds. It is up to us to use it.

A third poison on the tips of some of Satan's arrows is meant to nurture discouragement: both discouragement with one's personal life and discouragement with the organized church. The enemy has multiple opportunities to hit believers in both areas, it seems. Consider King David, an example of discouragement that was personal. With King Saul hot on his heels, the king spoke freely in Psalm 18 of his *"distress"* (v 6) and of the *"deep waters"* (v 16) he was going through. Then, all of a sudden, he remembered to exercise his faith. A few verses later we read of Satan's defeat. *"You gave me your shield of victory, and your right hand sustains me,"* David said, crediting the Lord with his release from spiritual depression (v 35).

Arrows aimed at discouragement with the organized church may not be as easy to deflect. Because we Christians belong to a kingdom that, in its widest definition, includes both wheat and tares, possessors and professors, the saved and the lost, there are times when the unbelievers among us seem to be winning the war. When this is the case, the Bible tells us to fight. Jude, in his short but passionate epistle, says, *"I felt I had to write and urge you to contend for the faith that was once for all entrusted to the saints,"* (v 3). The apostle Paul exhorts Timothy, *"The Spirit clearly says that in later times some will abandon the faith and follow deceiving spirits and things taught by demons....If you point these things out to the brothers, you will be a good minister of Christ Jesus brought up in the truths of the faith and of the good teaching you have followed"* (1 Timothy 4:1,6). The apostle John caps the discussion with his own endorsement of using one's "shield." *"This is the victory that has overcome the world, even our faith,"* he says (1 John 5:4).

So faith is the weapon that stops discouragement from consuming us. It seems to stop other negative emotions as well. But it is up to us to exercise the faith we have been given. It is up to us to look the enemy in the eye and declare, "You can have no victory over me, Satan. I am standing on fact, not on feeling. And I will proceed through life accordingly, to the praise and honor of my Lord."

THE HELMET OF SALVATION

After the soldier has picked up his shield, he reaches for his helmet. Once his head is protected, his suit of armor is complete. For the Christian there is a warning here. We are to guard our minds from thoughts that would cause us harm.

What this "helmet" is and why it is associated with "salvation" is interesting. The word "salvation" in its largest sense, connotes deliverance from all kinds of evil. Since temptation begins in the mind, this seems to be the logical place to defeat it—and to do so before an evil thought turns into action and delivers consequences that are devastating. "*Each one is tempted when by his own evil desire he is dragged away and enticed,*" James says. "*Then, after sin has conceived, it gives birth to sin; and sin, when it is full-grown, gives birth to death*" (James 1:14,15). This "death" could refer to the Christian's testimony, or it could be "death" of the unbeliever's soul. Whichever, the helmet of salvation provides protection.

How do we Christians put on our helmets? The Bible suggests practicing scriptural thought-control. "*The weapons we fight with are not the weapons of the world,*" the apostle Paul points out in his second letter to the Corinthians. "*On the contrary, they have divine power to demolish strongholds. We demolish arguments and every pretension that sets itself up against the knowledge of God, and we take captive every thought to make it obedient to Christ*" (2 Corinthians 10:4,5). Yes, wrong thoughts can become "*strongholds.*" But we can knock down these "*strongholds,*" the Bible says, by controlling what we think about. To do so, however, we have to don our helmets of salvation and keep them on every day of our lives.

There is an old proverb that goes like this: "You can't stop the birds from flying over your head, but you can stop them from making a nest in your hair." This means that although we do not have the power to keep evil thoughts from making their way into our heads—what we Christians find ourselves thinking about can be shocking—we can control what we do with those thoughts. Will we choose to dwell on them, or will we dismiss them? If we dismiss them, we will have victory. If we do not dismiss them, we will experience defeat.

We know, of course, that a mind that has been emptied can be a dangerous thing. Getting rid of one evil thought can pave the way for more evil thoughts to take its place. That is why God tells us to replace thoughts that are evil with thoughts that are good—thoughts that are *"true, noble, right, pure, lovely, admirable, excellent, or praiseworthy."* If we do this, *"the God of peace"* will be with us, the Bible says (see Philippians 4:8,9).

TWO OFFENSIVE WEAPONS

The *"sword of the Spirit"* is the last weapon the Christian soldier reaches for, yet in many ways, it is one of his most important. It is impossible to win the war against Satan without it. Every believer knows this. His *"sword"* is his Bible, the instrument that God describes as *"living, active, and sharper"* than any physical double-edged sword.

Its penetrating power is so effective it can divide *"soul and spirit, joints and marrow,"* we are told. It can even judge *"the thoughts and attitudes of the heart"* (see Hebrews 4:12,13).

As he is carrying the wisdom of the Bible into battle, the Christian is praying for victory, for prayer is the other offensive weapon he knows he cannot do without. If there is one thing Satan dreads more than anything else, it is meeting a Bible-believing person of prayer. "This person is in communication with God!" he says to himself. "This person is getting minute-by-minute instructions on how to handle himself! This person could blow apart my entire strategy! So Satan turns away from that particular Christian and moves on to a more vulnerable target.

Yes, the Bible gives instructions as to how to defeat Satan when he strikes us directly. But what if Satan works indirectly? What if he targets us through friends and associates, even through fellow-believers? Can we have victory over how our old nature tells us to respond? I believe so. Stay tuned.

Chapter 17

OVERCOME EVIL WITH FORGIVENESS AND LOVE

"[D]o not give the devil a foothold....Get rid of all bitterness, rage and anger, brawling and slander, along with every form of malice... forgiving each other, just as in Christ God forgave you."

—Ephesians 4:27,31,32

Several years ago I received a call from the Protestant Women of the Chapel at Fort Knox, Kentucky. My contact person said there was so much evil in the world that their group felt they needed a seminar on forgiveness. Would I fly down in the fall and minister to them? I said I would.

Excited, I grabbed a Bible, a pen and a blank sheet of paper. Then I sat down at my kitchen table. My goal was to come up with a working definition of forgiveness. It had to be God's definition, not somebody else's, I decided, and it had to spell out what the Bible requires us earthlings to *do* when we forgive someone. Three hours later I was still at the kitchen table, and my paper was still blank. This was going to be a challenging assignment!

At the time, Lee and I were team-teaching a large Bible class. Many minds are more efficient than a few, I figured. So I turned the challenge of finding a definition of forgiveness over to our students. They ended up struggling with it, too, until one member suggested it might be easier if we first determined what forgiveness is *not*. Her reasoning worked. What follows is a sampling of the Bible class's findings.

WHAT FORGIVENESS IS NOT

Forgiveness is not necessarily related to emotion. "I don't feel like forgiving," people say. If you wait until you feel like it, the class decided, you may be waiting forever. The unforgiving heart longs to retaliate: "Get the revenge that is due you! Demand the pound of flesh you deserve!" The problem is, seeking vengeance takes a huge toll, especially on the one doing the seeking.

Forgiveness is not conditional. When we say we are forgiving someone, we cannot use words like "if" or "but." The statement, "I'll forgive you if you promise never to do it again," places the offender in an impossible bind. And "I'm going to forgive you, but you will have to prove you deserve my forgiveness" ends up invalidating the very meaning of the word "forgiveness." Thankfully, God does not put conditions on the repentant sinner. If He did, who of us could stand before Him?

Forgiveness is not excusing the wrong. We cannot rationalize away an offense by saying, "He couldn't help it," when we know he could. And we cannot diminish the gravity of an incident by saying, "After all, she's only human." Breaches in relationships are serious—so serious God tells us to resolve them before approaching Him in worship (see Matthew 5:23,24).

Forgiveness is not smoothing things over. It is not saying to ourselves, "Everything will be fine" when we know otherwise. God does not trivialize sin, and we should not do so either. After all, sin is what sent His Son to the cross. A casual dismissal like "No problem" is something our heavenly Father would never say.

Forgiveness is not ignoring the incident. Some people treat relationship breaches as if they never happened. This is as foolish as making believe an arm that has been broken is still functional. If, however, the person with the dangling arm acknowledges the break, consults a physician, has the bone set (as painful as that process might be) and lets time heal it, the arm will end up being stronger in the place of the break than it was before the accident happened. This is welcome news for the Christian who has access to the greatest Physician of all, the Lord Jesus Christ.

Forgiveness is not simply forgetting. The human brain is a complicated computer, capable of storing a lifetime of memories. If the offense against us was a major one, like rape or sexual abuse, the murder of a loved one, spousal adultery, a financial swindle, or a vicious character attack, chances are we will not be able to forget it, no matter how hard we try. What we can do, however, is to file the incident under the "Do Not Retrieve!" part of our brains and leave it there.

This is what the Lord does with the evil deeds His followers commit against Him. He makes a vow not to retrieve them. As a result, when we meet Him in glory, He will not say, "I can't remember anything about your past." Rather, He is more likely to declare, "The sins you committed against Me deserve eternal damnation. But because my Son paid for them on the cross, I will never bring them up against you. You are a sinner who has been forgiven."

Is it not this grace that makes heaven so precious? Both parties are aware of the cost of healing a broken relationship. One paid that cost. The other has received the benefits. Talk about gratitude; we will feel it! Talk about mercy; we will be experiencing it! And talk about love, we will be the recipients of it! Eternally.

"Their sins and lawless acts I will remember no more," the Lord says of His people (Hebrews 10:17). *"[A]s far as the east is from the west, so far has he removed our transgressions from us,"* the forgiven psalmist declares (Psalm 103:12). *"[Y]ou hurl all our iniquities into the depths of the sea,"* the prophet Micah exults (Micah 7:19). Thankfully, on the spot where our sins were lowered God has erected a "No Fishing" sign.

So, using our Lord's forgiveness as an example, we might draw the following conclusions: If by "forget" we mean "an inability to remember what happened," then we cannot use "forgive" and "forget" in the same sentence. If, however, by "forget" we mean "a conscious decision not to bring up the past," either as a weapon against the offender or as a personal reminder of the pain we ourselves have endured, then we can utter "forgive" and "forget" in the same breath. It should be added that if an unpleasant incident is not revisited for a long period of time, certain details of what happened may become fuzzy. Who knows? Perhaps after a few years the whole thing, depending on its degree of seriousness, may have been truly "forgotten." Our heavenly Father is a merciful and compassionate God.

WHAT FORGIVENESS IS

After coming up with this list of "What Forgiveness Is Not," our Bible class was able to formulate a working definition of what forgiveness is. It went as follows: "Forgiveness is an act of the will, made possible by the grace of God, whereby we throw away our list of grievances and release the offender from payment." The class took care to support each portion of its definition with Scripture. Here are a few of the verses they dug out of God's Word:

AN ACT OF THE WILL

Forgiveness is an action, not a feeling. It is something we *do*. We do it because God has commanded us to do it. The Bible says, *"Therefore, as God's chosen people, holy and dearly loved, clothe yourselves with compassion, kindness, humility, gentleness, and patience. Bear with each other and forgive whatever grievances you may have against one another. Forgive as the Lord forgave you"* (Colossians 3:12,13). Notice the imperatives.

Before God comes into our lives and gives us the where-withal to *"clothe"* ourselves with *"compassion,"* things like bitterness, malice, rancor, and resentment consume us. Getting rid of these destructive influences requires us to *do* something: to *"forgive"* our offenders as God has forgiven us, *His* offenders. Then the destructive influences flee.

GOD'S ENABLING GRACE

Without the grace of God there can be no forgiveness at all, at least not as God defines the word. Biblical forgiveness is made possible only when we come to the understanding that the grace which has been poured on us from heaven is expected to continue its journey through us to others. God provides the wherewithal. We become the conduits.

Can the conduits ever hinder the flow of God's grace? we wonder. Listen to what the author of Hebrews writes: *"Be careful that none of you fails to respond to the grace which God gives, for if he does there can very easily spring up in him a bitter spirit, which is not only bad in itself but can also poison the lives of many others"* (Hebrews 12:14,15 Phillips).

If we are failing *"to respond to the grace which God gives,"* either by enjoying the fact that we have been thoroughly victimized or by reveling in the pain we are inflicting on our offenders, perhaps it is time for a heart examination. Dr. Martin Lloyd Jones looks at his own spiritual chest x-ray and asks, "How do I know if my sins are forgiven?" Then he answers this way: "If I am forgiving others."

The Great Physician agrees. *"For if you forgive men when they sin against you, your heavenly Father will also forgive you,"* He told His disciples. *"But if you do not forgive men their sins, your Father will not forgive your sins"* (Matthew 6:14,15).

TOSSING AWAY THAT LIST OF GRIEVANCES

A person who keeps tallies of offenses, either in his head or on paper, has not forgiven his offenders. The Bible's most famous discourse on love (First Corinthians, chapter thirteen) points out (in many different translations and paraphrases) how different our idea of love is from God's. His kind of love *"keeps no record (or score) of wrongs,"* we learn (1 Corinthians13:5, NIV & NEB). It *"does not hold grudges"* (TLB). It *"does not take into account the wrong suffered"* (NAS). And it *"takes no account of the evil done to it"* (AMP). In other words, if we want to love others as Christ loves us, our list of grievances must go.

RELEASING THE OFFENDER FROM PAYMENT

Pressing our so-called right to retaliate is another indication that forgiveness has not yet taken place. This lesson is taught in the eighteenth chapter of Matthew's gospel through the story of two people who have incurred debts. One debt is canceled; the other is not. Here is how the story goes: A gentleman we will call A forgives B a tremendous amount of money, releasing him from paying his debt. B, however, demands payment of C, who owes him a mere pittance in comparison. When C cannot satisfy his debt, B has him *"thrown into prison"* (v 30). When A hears what has happened to C, he upbraids B for his lack of compassion. *"I canceled all that debt of yours because you begged me to,"* he says. *"Shouldn't you have had mercy on your fellow servant just as I had on you?"* (v 33).

As a result of his refusal to forgive, B ends up in prison, too, where he is *"tortured,"* the Bible says (v 34). It is a prison of his own making, in a sense, because he has refused to surrender his claim to retaliate against C. Jesus, who is the narrator of this story, makes a sobering statement: *"This is how my heavenly Father will treat each of you unless you forgive your brother from your heart"* (v 35). The conclusion to the matter seems to be that the drive to exact payment imprisons both the offender and the offended, whereas the act of forgiveness can release both.

Once the class came up with this last segment of its definition, I was relieved. I was ready for that seminar in Fort Knox, I felt. How wrong I was!

HELP FROM A FRIEND

I decided to try out my understanding of forgiveness on a dear pastor friend of ours, Stan Rockafellow. As I recited the words our class members had come up with, Stan listened intently. Then he said, "It's a great definition, Peg—as far as it goes."

"What do you mean 'as far as it goes'?" I asked, remembering the hard work that had gone into that definition.

"Well, you have to add one more phrase. You have to say, 'and without malice or judgment, willingly bear the consequences of the offender's actions.'"

"You're kidding!" I exclaimed. "What do you mean?"

"Well," Stan answered, "if you want to follow in the steps of the Lord, you must take care to do what He did. He paid the debt we sinners owed, and He did it by suffering the hell we sinners deserved. Furthermore, He did it willingly, without harboring malice and without passing judgment."

"How does that translate horizontally?" I asked.

"It translates into your becoming the offender's sin-bearer," he explained. "You have to be willing, for the sake of the gospel, to face consequences befitting the offender, not you, the offended—consequences like cold stares, behind-the-back whispers, outright blame, or any other behavior designed to humiliate. Having to endure the consequences of a sin your offender deserves (and you do not) can seem like 'hell' at times. But the hardest part may come when you make an attempt at reconciliation and are ridiculed for it, perhaps even mocked. When this happens, you know you are carrying out forgiveness God's way."

"I can't forgive like that!" I exclaimed. "There is no way in this world I am going to suffer the consequences of my offender's sin! What do I do if I can't forgive?"

There was silence.

The Kentucky engagement was now only a week away, and I was stymied. I realized I could not address this issue of forgiveness without an answer to my question. It was a question that, by this time, was screaming at me.

God had the answer, I knew. And He would give it to me. But how? I noticed that next to the chair I was sitting in was a stack of books a friend had given me that morning, so I picked up the top one and opened it. A Scripture verse was staring me in the face. The longer I looked at it, the bigger it got. Soon the letters seemed larger than the book itself. It was my answer! And it was hidden in the context of Moses' having led the Israelites to Marah, where the water was too bitter to drink. Moses did not know what to do, so he took his problem to the Lord. *"[T]he Lord showed him a tree,"* the Bible says, *"and he threw it into the water and the water became sweet"* (Exodus 15:25).

I knew immediately what the tree represented. It represented the cross. Jesus died on a "tree," I remembered. This "tree" had the power to make the "bitter waters" of life fresh again. If we are faithful to do what we can do (throw in the tree), the Bible seemed to be saying, the Lord will do what we cannot do (provide the power to forgive). The ability to forgive lies in Him, not in us. *Yes!*

LEE, COME HERE!

I was so excited about discovering the answer to my question—and just in the nick of time—that I called out to Lee who was in another room. He came running.

"Do you know what you're supposed to do when you can't forgive somebody?" I asked. "You're supposed to *'throw in the tree!'*"

"I thought you were supposed to throw in the towel," he laughed.

"That's giving up," I replied. "Throwing in the tree is giving over." I recounted Moses' story, ending with the tossing of the branch into the water and its miraculous result. Lee was quiet for a moment, then he mused, "It seems to me, Peg, that when you throw in the tree, you have to climb on it."

Now it was my turn to be quiet. I knew exactly what my husband meant. We who have been offended have to "die"—die to self, die to pride, die to what we would like to see happen in the life of the offender. On that "tree" is a place for every part of the body: a place for the mind (Will I think only positive thoughts about him/her?), a place for the eyes (Will I look upon the offender as God does?), a place for the ears (Will I filter out the nasty things that are being said?), a place for the mouth (Will I speak the truth in love?), a place for the heart (Will I replace bitterness with forgiveness?), a place for the hands (Will I determine to reach out in compassion?), a place for the knees (Will I pray for this one who is despitefully using me?), and a place for the feet (Will I take that first step toward reconciliation?).

WHAT ABOUT RECONCILIATION?

Unfortunately, we have to face the fact that we may do all the things that God requires without experiencing restoration in the relationship that has been broken. In fact, the relationship could get worse. The offender may not only refuse to reconcile, he may drive more "nails" into us.

"How long do I have to stay on this cross?" we cry in desperation.

"Until you are dead," the Spirit replies.

"How will I know when I'm dead?" we ask, not really expecting an answer.

"When it doesn't hurt anymore," He says.

Then He adds, "But don't get discouraged. You have to 'die' in order to live, remember? Death to self is your route to resurrection power. Whether or not your broken relationship gets mended diminishes in importance in comparison to what God wants to do in your life. He wants to make you like His Son, causing you to rise to new life in Him. He wants you to leave the task of judging others to the Father. *'It is mine to avenge; I will repay,'* the Father says. *'If your enemy is hungry, feed him; if he is thirsty, give him something to drink...Do not be overcome by evil, but overcome evil with good'"* (Romans 12:19–21).

"Who knows? Perhaps by your *'good behavior in Christ'* (1 Peter 3:16), your offender may become *'ashamed'* of himself and return to the *'Shepherd and Overseer of [his] soul,'* asking God's forgiveness of his sins (see 1 Peter 2:21–25). That would be the ultimate reward of *your* forgiveness, wouldn't it—one well worth suffering for?"

EPILOGUE

Did I board the plane to Fort Knox? I did. Were my lectures on forgiveness well received? They were. In fact, many more seminars followed as a result. I never feel as if I have this forgiveness message all put together though, either in content or in personal application. It is a subject that is huge, and learning to live in the power of Christ's resurrection is a daily discipline, especially when the persecution being experienced is for one's faith. We Christians know where our victory lies, however. It lies in the Lord Jesus Christ. He is our all in all. Let us be reminded of this glorious fact again. Please join me for the next and final chapter.

Chapter 18

Learn to Live in Christ's Victory

"With God we will gain the victory, and he will trample down our enemies."

—Psalm 60:12

What if 9/11 happens again? What if the attacks are worse this time? What if Christians are targeted specifically? What if imprisonment and torture are in our future? What if....

We believers fret about such things, but should we? After all, what is the essence of life? Is it physical or spiritual? Were we placed in this world to be safe or to be sanctified? Did Jesus Christ die to save us from our trials or from our sins? Is our existence about the here and now or about forever?

The Word of God has much to say about suffering and persecution. Listen to a few verses on the subject. *"Consider it pure joy, my brothers, whenever you face trials of many* kinds," James says, *"because you know that the testing of your faith develops perseverance"* (James 1:2,3). *"Whatever happens, conduct yourselves in a manner worthy of the gospel of Christ,"* the apostle Paul adds, *"...without being frightened in any way by those who oppose you....For it has been granted to you on behalf of Christ not only to believe on him, but also to suffer for him..."* (Philippians 1:27–29). Jesus Himself sums up the subject of suffering by saying, *"Blessed are you when people insult you, persecute you and falsely say all kinds of evil against you because of me. Rejoice and be glad, because great is your reward in heaven..."* (Matthew 5:11,12).

THINK BACK

Difficulties in life are nothing new. From the very beginning, people have had their share of troubles. *"Dear friends,"* the apostle Peter admonished early believers, *"do not be surprised at the painful trial you are suffering, as though some strange thing were happening to you. But rejoice that you participate in the sufferings of Christ, so that you may be overjoyed when his glory is revealed. If you are insulted because of the name of Christ, you are blessed, for the Spirit of glory and of God rests on you"* (1 Peter 4:12–14). The apostle believed Christians are *"called"* to suffer. It is part of their identification with their Lord. If they want to experience His victory, they have to go His route. They have to *"follow in his steps,"* as Peter put it (1 Peter 2:21).

Christ's *"steps,"* we know from studying His life, led downward before they led upward. The Savior had to be born, to suffer, to die, and to be buried before He could experience resurrection, ascension, being seated at His Father's right hand, and returning to the earth as King of kings. His route included the distasteful as well as the delightful.

Our route, by design, is similar. The apostle Paul knew this. He yearned for identification with His Savior. *"I want to know Christ and the power of his resurrection and the fellowship of sharing in his sufferings, becoming like him in his death, and so, somehow, to attain to the resurrection from the dead,"* he said (Philippians 3:10).

This is my own desire, too. In fact, I chose the above portion of Scripture long ago to be my "life's verse," wishing initially that I could shorten it to say, *"I want to know Christ and the power of his resurrection,"* period! But the older I get, the more I want to recite the whole thing. I want to go all the way with my Lord. "All the way" may mean experiencing *"the fellowship of sharing in his sufferings"* as well as in His victories. I know that. I keep reminding myself there is no excuse for wanting to skip over a necessary segment of the Christian walk just because it happens to be unpleasant or painful.

How the Identification Principle Works

We Christians begin our identification with the Savior the minute we are *"born again"* (see John 3:3–8). This is the point at which we put aside glorifying self and step into a brand new life. Our new life is dedicated to bringing glory to the Lord and to Him alone.

Suffering is bound to follow new birth. This suffering, which includes all things unpleasant, can also include persecution. After all, anybody who professes to be a believer in Christ invites the wrath of non-believers, who, whether they are willing to admit it or not, have a deep-seated hatred of the Lord (John 15:18). *"If they persecuted me,"* Jesus warned His disciples, *"they will persecute you also"* (v 20). In other words, they will take out their distaste for God on you, His earthly representative. They will do this because they are uncomfortable with the positive life-change that Jesus Christ has made in this person they thought they knew. The change makes them, by comparison, look bad. Unfortunately, opportunities for non-believers to act out their rage on believers are multiplied in this age of globalization and ethnic mingling.

The type of persecution Christians face varies with the circumstances they find themselves in. Some persecution is emotional; other is physical. But the end to which most persecutors work is the same: they want to destroy that annoying person who has a lifestyle that is threatening to theirs. Thankfully, God is able to override this destructive goal with a goal of His own.

Surprisingly, the Lord's goal is destruction, too, but the kind of destruction He wills is destruction of the Christian's old nature—destruction of self. Persecution can accomplish this goal. It can separate the chaff from the wheat, the trivial from the significant, the physical from the spiritual. It can also give Christians a deeper appreciation of the sufferings of Christ. It does this by showing them that the most glorious victories of all come after the most unbearable pain.

In order for Christians to claim Christ's victories, however, they have to walk all the way in the Savior's shoes. "All the way" includes dying to self. They have to come to that point in their lives where they throw up their hands, admit their weaknesses, forego their own agendas and submit to God's purposes. *"Father, if you are willing, take this cup from me,"* Jesus cried; *"yet not my will but yours be done"* (Luke 22:42). Determination to carry out the Father's will, regardless of the awful cost, was a defining moment for the Savior. It can be the same for us.

For those of us living in the Western world, dying to self's desires is hard. We are surrounded by people bent on achieving health, wealth, and personal happiness—goals that are physical and transient. God's goal, in contrast, is to make us holy. He concentrates on that which is spiritual and eternal.

Not only do we Christians have to "die" to self in order to achieve God's goal of personal holiness; we also have to "bury" many of our sinful dreams. Imagine yourself bundling up those self-glorifying plans of yours, placing them in a box, bidding them farewell and lowering them into the ground. When the "funeral" is over—and *only* when the funeral is over—can your identification with Christ take its positive turn. Only then can you "rise" to new life in the Spirit. Only then can you "ascend" to the heavenlies and look upon your problems from God's perspective. Only then can you "sit" by your heavenly Father's side, and become an effective intercessor for people you know. And only then can you "return" to your own heartaches and sufferings and face them head on, knowing that victory is yours.

DESTRUCTION OF LIFE'S "LAST ENEMY"

Death to self (a spiritual event) and death to the body (a physical event) are two different things. When we talk about being identified with Christ, we are talking primarily about an identification that is spiritual. This means that most of our victories will be spiritual in nature, at least right now. Physical suffering and physical death will still be with us. Everybody will experience pain, and most of us will die. The only people who get to escape physical death are those believers who are alive when Jesus Christ returns. They will be *"caught up"*…to meet the Lord *"in the air,"* the Bible says, never having known what it is to die in a physical sense (1 Thessalonians 4:17). The rest of us, however, will meet the grim reaper face to face.

Some of us will die young, and others will reach old age. Some will expire gently; others, violently. Some will leave this world alone, and others will be surrounded by loved ones. Whichever way we go, one thing is sure: for those of us who know the Lord Jesus Christ, our deaths will be *"precious"* (see Psalm 116:15). The Savior Himself will be with us, leading us onward. He will walk us *"through the valley of the shadow of death"* (Psalm 23:4). And once we clear the valley, He will present us *"without fault"* to His heavenly Father—a ceremony He will perform *"with great joy,"* the Bible says (Jude 24).

Physical death, by biblical definition, involves a separation of the spirit from the body. While the believer's remains are being washed, dressed, viewed, and buried, his/her spirit is already enjoying eternal bliss with the Savior. To be *"away from the body"* is to be *"at home with the Lord,"* the Bible teaches (2 Corinthians 5:8).

When does the spirit enter glory? you ask. Immediately. With the body's last breath. The spirit's instant transfer is assured because of what happened many years ago on a hill called Calvary. There Jesus paid sin's penalty in full. No additional payment is required. As a result, Christians have been granted direct access to the place that will be their eternal home.

The body, in contrast to the spirit, is relegated to the grave. *"[F]or dust you are and to dust you will return,"* the Bible says (Genesis 3:19). The body will stay in the ground (or in an alternative resting place) until the Second Coming of Jesus Christ. At that time *"all who are in their graves will hear his voice and come out—those who have done good will rise to live, and those who have done evil will rise to be condemned"* (John 5:28,29). When the bodies of Christians rise, they will be *"clothed with immortality,"* the Bible says, and reunited with their corresponding spirits, which are already in glory, awaiting completion. When the body and spirit come together once again, this time in a union that is both permanent and perfect, death will have been *"swallowed up in victory."* Life's last enemy will have been destroyed, never to plague God's people again (See 1 Corinthians 15:51–57).

BEFORE-DEATH CHALLENGES

"It's not death that troubles me," I have heard Christians say; "it's what comes *before* death. I'm not coping very well with aging, so how will I handle dying? And if before I die, I get tortured for my faith—God forbid—I wonder how I will fare."

You will fare well, I believe. In fact, you will fare well whatever happens to you, for God is in all of it. Let us consider God's grace in the aging process first. Believe it or not, growing older does have its positive side. In addition to the experience and wisdom the advancing years bring, there is the sweet realization that every day brings us closer to heaven. Watching these bodies of ours deteriorate can make us more willing than ever to leave them. Think about it. When the foundations of a house start to crumble, the supports begin to buckle, the hinges creak like crazy, the plumbing starts leaking, the electrical wiring shorts out, the thermostats break down, the sound system no longer works, the windows cloud up, and the roof top is getting thin, we are more apt to consider moving. "I'm out of here!" we exclaim. For Christians, there is a brand new house just waiting—one with no mortgage to pay. As for me, I can hardly wait for "moving day." The idea of starting over with everything new and "free" is very appealing to me.

I must admit, however, that watching the body deteriorate can be a challenge. Add suffering, persecution, and possible torture to normal physical decline, and the strongest among us get concerned. Jesus told His disciples their greatest fear should be not of what can happen to the body but of what might happen to the soul. He warned against renouncing one's faith under persecution. "*All this I have told you so that you will not go astray…,*" He said. "*[A] time is coming when anyone who kills you will think he is offering a service to God. They will do such things because they have not known the Father or me. I have told you this so that when the time comes, you will remember that I told you"* (John 16:1–4).

GOD'S GRACE TO THE RESCUE

But what if we fail God's test? we wonder.

"My grace is sufficient for you," God answers, *"for my power is made perfect in weakness"* (2 Corinthians 12:9). Although we may not possess the wherewithal to endure suffering, persecution, or torture right now, God's grace will be there when we need it. It reminds me of a story the late Corrie ten Boom used to tell about the time when, as a young girl, she asked her father to give her her ticket for the approaching train and to do so "now!" Her father told her he would indeed give her the ticket, but not until the train pulled into the station. So it is with our heavenly Father. He gives us the grace we need when we need it. Not before.

God's delay is not to be confused with a refusal. God's grace is a sure thing. Listen to what the apostle Paul said about facing *his* uncertain future. (The words mean more when we realize he had already endured imprisonments, floggings, canings, stonings, a shipwreck, sleeplessness, hunger, cold, nakedness, and many other hardships for his faith—see 2 Corinthians 11:24–27). *"Who shall separate us from the love of Christ?"* he asked. *"Shall trouble or hardship or persecution or famine or nakedness or danger or sword?... No, in all these things we are more than conquerors through him who loved us. For I am convinced that neither death nor life, neither angels nor demons, neither the present nor the future, nor any powers, neither height nor depth, nor anything else in all creation, will be able to separate us from the love of God that is in Christ Jesus our Lord"* (Romans 8:35–39).

This is a rather emphatic and comprehensive statement, is it not? But the most important thing about it is this: It is true! Evil can strip us of a lot of things—things we dearly love. But it cannot strip us of God's love. That will be there forever, no matter what happens. It will be there to comfort us, to nourish us, to encourage us, and to give us victory, especially in the hour of trial.

The battle with evil has already been won. The Conqueror's flag has already been raised in triumph. The Victor's boot has already been placed on the neck of the vanquished. And the enemy's soldiers even now are being led as captives through the streets.

Do I hear shouts of joy? Of course I do. Are Christians grabbing each other in caring abandon? Most certainly they are. Is there going to be a celebration? Yes, there is. Do not miss it, my friend. Come, join us. You will receive a warm welcome in the company of the people God calls His "redeemed." This is a group of people who know what it means to live in victory. It is a victory Christ died to purchase for them. And the group always has room for one more.

STUDY GUIDE/
DISCUSSION QUESTIONS

PART ONE:
POINTS TO PONDER: A STUDY OF EVIL

Chapter 1: Evil Reigns—or Does it?

1. Where were you on 9/11? What emotions did you experience as the events of that day unfolded? What Scripture verses, if any, came to mind?

2. Read the following Bible passages, answering the questions that accompany them:

    • Psalm 10: What parts of this psalm bless you? What parts trouble you? Do you feel it is appropriate to call for God's vengeance on one's enemies? Explain your answer.

    • Psalm 60:1–4: The psalmist attributes the troubles of his day to the Lord's doing. Some people do the same with the events of 9/11. In your estimation, was 9/11 a wake-up call from

God to our nation, or was it simply an evil attack perpetuated by wicked men? Could it have been both? Explain your answer.

- Psalm 64: What section of this psalm makes a good prayer? What section is an accurate description of present-day terrorists? What section is encouraging to Christians?

3. Relate a time when you had the opportunity to tell someone the sovereign Lord is still on His throne (See Psalm 103:19). How was your witness received? How does a person's view of God affect his/her ability to face trials? How can we help people who have a wrong view of God find out what God is really like?

4. In this chapter the author mentions three redeeming features of tragedies. Name them. Which one speaks most powerfully to you? Why?

Chapter 2: Evil Emerged in Eden—or Was It Earlier?

1. Read Genesis 3. What must it have been like for Adam and Eve before the Fall? What temptations were present in the Garden? Who sinned? What choices did each participant in sin make? Whose will dictated each choice? What areas of life and what personal relationships were affected by the bad choices made in the Garden? Give a present-day example of the devastating effects sin can have on a life.

2. How did God show His displeasure with what Adam and Eve had done? What gracious act did the Lord perform for Adam and Eve that foreshadowed what He would do for future believers in Jesus Christ? Why did Adam and Eve need a protective covering? Why do we?

3. The author mentions three possibilities of when and where evil may have had its origins. Restate the three possibilities in your own words. Based on your knowledge of God and of Scripture, which time and place for evil's origin do you find most defensible? Why?

4. Why, when studying evil, is it important to understand what the Bible says about God and His workings? What attribute(s) of God does each of the following verses highlight and how does each attribute determine how God relates to evil: Psalms 90:2, Hebrews 4:13, Psalms 104:24, Psalm 86:5, Exodus 15:11, Psalm 89:14, Numbers 23:19, Job 42:2?

5. What lessons can we learn from Satan's attempt to be like God? How can we avoid repeating Satan's sin of elevating himself to god-like status? Why is it important to remember who we are in relation to who God is? What happens if we don't? (See Matthew 23:12.)

Chapter 3: Evil Serves Satan—Does It Also Serve God?

1. In this chapter, the author uses the analogy of how a symphony is constructed to show the value of contrasts. Think of another analogy that could have been used. Relate a time in your life when you came to appreciate the value of contrasts.

2. Why is it important to know that life's "symphony" ends triumphantly? What if it didn't? If you were writing an opera entitled, "God's Plan of Redemption from Beginning to End," what would be your first scene? What other scenes would you include? How would you want your drama to end? (In answering,

describe the lighting, costumes, soloists, scenery, and music, etc.)

3. Do you agree or disagree with authors Bayne and Hinlicky, who assert that it is "easier to accept a world spun out of control, with evil abounding, than a world ordered by God where evil has a chosen place"? What is it about the concept of evil's having a "chosen place" that makes people uncomfortable? What aspect of the concept of evil's having a "chosen place" in God's plan brings comfort?

4. Why is it spiritually beneficial for a believer to subscribe to the following truths: 1) that God is in control of all things and 2) that Satan is limited in what he can do? By the way, what are some of Satan's limits?

5. If you were trying to convince someone that things on earth, as horrible as they sometimes are, are ultimately going according to plan, which of the following Scripture verses would you find most useful and why: Isaiah 46:8–11, Romans 11:32, Ephesians 1:3–14, and Revelation 13:8?

Chapter 4: Evil Turns Good People Bad—or Are All Bad from the Start?

1. Describe a time when you watched a child's sin nature manifest itself. What was your reaction? What were the reactions of the child's parent(s)? After reading Romans 3:9–20, what would you say is the primary responsibility of a parent?

2. Comment on the following quotation from Reinhold Neibuhr: "Most of the evil in this world comes not from evil people. It comes from people who consider themselves good." Relate a time in history when a

person or a nation was duped because the goodness of humanity was wrongly assumed. Is it possible to be too hard on human nature? Why or why not?

3. A holocaust survivor is quoted as saying, "I saw [in Eichmann] the capacity in myself to do the same thing." After reading Jeremiah 17:9, how do you think the prophet would have reacted to the Holocaust survivor's statement? After reading Matthew 15:19, how do you think Jesus would have reacted? For whom were Jesus' harshest words reserved?

4. The Bible makes a contrast between those outside of Christ and those "in" Christ. From phrases used in Ephesians 2, fill in the blanks below:

Life Before Christ	*Life After Christ*
a. "Dead in trespasses and sins" (v1)	a. "Made _____ with Christ" (v5)
b. "Objects of wrath" (v3)	b. Objects of God's great _____ and rich _____ (v4)
c. Serving "the ruler of the kingdom of the air" (v2)	c. Enjoying fellowship with "_____ in the _____" (v6)
d. Pursuing salvation by "works" (v9)	d. Receiving salvation by "_____" (v8)
e. "Foreigners to the covenants of the promise" (v12)	e. "Fellow citizens with God's _____ and members of God's _____." (v19)

f. "Without God" (v12)

f. "A dwelling in which
_____" (v22)

g. "Far away" (v13)

g. "Brought _____
through the blood of
Christ" (v13)

h. Alienated from God
by a "dividing wall of
hostilities" (v14)

h. "Granted _____ to
the Father by one Spirit"
(v18)

Chapter 5: There Are Many Classes of People—or Are There Only Two?

1. What event(s) in the life of Jonah caused the prophet to call the Lord *"a gracious and compassionate God"* (Jonah 4:2)? Relate a time when God gave you a second chance. How did you feel after that experience? According to Hebrews 9:27, when do second chances cease?

2. Given the fact that God *"takes no pleasure in the death of anyone"* (Ezekiel 18:32), explain why the Father in heaven condemns unredeemed sinners to hell. The gospel of Matthew pictures Jesus weeping over those who refuse to come to Him (23:37). What does this picture tell us about the Savior? What does it tell us about the lost? Using terminology found in Romans 2:5–11, describe the person who will experience God's wrath.

3. The author reminds us that the Bible divides people into two categories: the "unsaved" and the "saved." Why is there no category for the "almost saved"? Using language found in John 3, describe these two categories of people in other ways. In order for a person to go from being "unsaved" to "saved," what

divine action must take place? What human action must accompany this divine action?

4. From the following Scriptures, describe hell: Matthew 8:12, Isaiah 66:24, Luke 16:22–24, 2 Thessalonians 1:6–10, and Daniel 12:2,3. In your opinion, which characteristic of hell would be the hardest to endure? Why? According to John 3:16–18, how can one escape eternal damnation?

Chapter 6: A Cry from Hell (a Dramatization of What Evildoers Face)

1. Explain why an appreciation for God's love is deepened when viewed in light of God's wrath. Why is it dangerous to accentuate one divine attribute over another?

2. Describe the emotions you felt as you listened to the woman speaking from hell. What changes occurred in her during the course of the drama? What did *not* change? According to Isaiah 55:11, God's Word achieves the purpose for which He sends it. Tell how this truth applies to people in hell.

3. The situation with the rich man and Lazarus, described in Luke 16:19–31, makes it clear it is impossible to go from hell to heaven. Why can there be no such "switch"? (In answering, consider both the character of God and the nature of humankind.)

4. It might be said, "Hell is final, yet it isn't." Use the following Scripture passages to elaborate on this statement: John 3:36, Matthew 8:12, Matthew 25:41, Revelation 20:10, and Revelation 21:8.

5. Read Matthew 7:21–23, which contains a description of people who are active about the Lord's business. At Judgment Day, He banishes these "churchgoers"

from His presence, calling them "evildoers." How do you account for this rejection? According to 2 Corinthians 13:5, what practical steps can true believers take to make sure this frightening fate never befalls them?

PART TWO:
SITUATIONS TO SCRUTINIZE:
EVIL IN BIBLE TIMES

Chapter 7: Excessive Evil in Noah's Day and God's Righteous Judgment

1. If you had been a TV reporter covering the catastrophic events of Noah's day, whom would you interview? What questions would you ask? What pictures would you direct your cameraman to take?
2. Read Matthew 24:37–39. Make a list of comparisons between the spiritual climate in our present day and that of Noah's day. When people sin frequently and excessively, how do you think God feels: wrathful? sad? disgusted? angry? disappointed? frustrated? hopeful? Explain your answers. What benefits come with acknowledging sin and repenting of it, both individually and nationally (See 1 John 1:9 and 2 Chronicles 7:14)?
3. Read Psalm 46. Notice the admonition to *"Be still and know that I am God"* (v 10). How is it possible to *"be still"* in the midst of a natural disaster (v 2)? What promises, do you imagine, sustained Noah and his family while the rains were pounding down? What

biblical promises have you clung to in your own times of need?

4. Describe a time when you were mocked for your faith. How did you react? If you had a chance to go back and "redo" your behavior, what changes, if any, would you make? How does it make you feel to know that mockers will receive their just desserts one day (See 2 Peter2:9)? Why is divine retribution an important part of God's plan?

5. Come up with a biblically sound, yet loving, response to the following remarks:
   - "I think their store burned down because they were open on Sundays."
   - "I'm mad at God. He could have kept my daughter from dying and He didn't."
   - "The tornado made me rethink my priorities. I'm going to church again."

Chapter 8: How Evil Targeted Joseph and Job and How God Used It for Good

1. Give some examples (either from the Bible, from history, or from current events) of situations in which innocent people were made to suffer. When we use the word "innocent" in situations like these, what do we mean and what do we *not* mean?

2. Share a time when you yourself were unfairly targeted. What evidence do you have that God's hand was on your adversary's "bow"? How did God work your heartache for your good and His glory?

3. What person(s) unfairly targeted Joseph and Job? How did each one of these patriarchs react to adversity? (What was similar? What was different?) How

did God turn each one of these men's problems into blessings?

4. Pain that comes from loss can impact us in many ways: emotionally, physically, economically, and spiritually. In which of these ways was Job affected when he 1) lost his animals, 2) lost his servants, 3) lost his health, 4) was taunted by his wife, and 5) was accused by his friends? Why do words sometimes hurt more than actions?

5. At the beginning of his troubles, Job complains about the *"arrows of the Almighty"* having hit him (6:4). By the end of his ordeal, Job is praising God for targeting him (42:1–6). What caused Job to change his perspective on his troubles? What, if any, practical steps can be taken to prepare oneself for suffering? For what kinds of tragedies can one never be totally prepared and why? Why do we need God to rescue us in times like these?

Chapter 9: King Saul's Evil Spirit from the Lord: a Possible Explanation

1. Consider the following questions, sparked by this chapter:

   • If all people are born with sin natures (Romans 3:11), how can they do any good deeds at all (obey parents, forgive wrongs, etc. as Saul did in his younger days)?

   • What specific sins did Saul commit that led to his demise?

   • In your estimation, how big a part did Satan play in Saul's downfall?

   • If someone asked you how an evil spirit can come from the Lord, what would you say?

- Why are Satan and his minions ultimately accountable to God for what they do?

2. At one point in Saul's life we're told that *"the Spirit of God came upon him in power, and he burned with anger"* (1 Samuel 11:6). How do you explain the following facts: 1) that Saul's anger, a characteristic not usually associated with godliness, came from God and 2) that God used Saul's *"burning anger"* to accomplish something good (1 Samuel 11:7)? In Deuteronomy 29:16–29 we read about a time when God Himself had a *"burning anger."* Why is righteous anger a necessary part of who God is?

3. In light of Jesus' actions, described in Mark 11:12–18, when is righteous anger called for? According to Galatians 5:16–26, when is anger sinful? From the following verses, list some practical steps Christians can take to avoid sinning when angry: Proverbs 22:24, Proverbs 29:11, 1 Corinthians 13:4–7, Ephesians 4:26,27; and James 1:19–21.

4. Read Deuteronomy 4:19, Deuteronomy 18:9–13, and Acts 16:16–18 and list some of the occult practices forbidden by God. What happened when Saul got involved with a medium? (see 1 Samuel 28.) What can we learn from Saul's encounter with the witch of Endor?

Chapter 10: King David's Flirtations with Evil and God's Gracious Forgiveness

1. Describe a time when you, like David, tried to cover one sin with another. What were the results? (Option: Describe a time when you tried to make a bad situation better and it only got worse.) What did you learn from your folly?

2. After reading the following Scriptures, state the positive role guilt played in David's life: Psalm 32:1–5,10; Psalm 38, Psalm 51. According to 1 John 1:9, what good can come from confessing one's sins? Why do some people feel guilty even after they have confessed their sins? How would you counsel such people?

3. Read Nathan's rebuke of David in 2 Samuel 12:1–25. What method did Nathan use to point out David's sin? Why was this approach more effective than blurting out, "David, you are a sinner. Get ready to pay. Big time!" Tell how each of David's four sons died: the baby (2 Samuel 12:15–19), Ammon (2 Samuel 13:22–33), Absalom (2 Samuel 18), and Adonijah (1 Kings 2:13–25). Which of these deaths were a fulfillment of 2 Samuel 12:10–12? In what ways did King David experience God's grace in the midst of his pain?

4. Why was David's numbering of his troops an offense to God? Why would Satan want to become involved in such a routine military operation as a census taking? What did God accomplish through David's misguided command? What can we learn from David's folly?

Chapter 11: Using Evil to Punish Evil: God's Unique Prerogative

1. What was your initial response when you read that God used evildoers to punish other evildoers, and then punished the evildoers that were carrying out His judgment for their own sins? What is surprising

about this divine method of operation? What is *not* surprising? What is comforting to the Christian?

2. The Bible says, *"From the one who has been entrusted with much, much more will be asked"* (Luke 12:48). Make a list of responsibilities with which God entrusted the Israelites. In what areas were they faithful to their trust? In what areas did they fail? What were some reasons for their failures?

3. Describe a time when you were entrusted with a responsibility you didn't (or couldn't) carry out. How did you feel? What lessons did you learn from your failure? What "trusts from God" are you currently concerned about administering well?

4. Read the account of the "Quail from the Lord" in Numbers 11:4–6, 18–20, 31–34; Psalm 78:17–31; and Psalm 106:13–15. Put yourself in God's place by recounting a time when, as a parent, you gave in to your child's nagging, knowing things would not turn out well for the child. Put yourself in God's place by recounting a time when, as a child, you nagged your parents, got what you asked for, and then wished you hadn't. In what ways was this sending of the quail a typical "parental response"? In what ways was it different? What lessons can Christians learn from the quail story?

5. Read Numbers 33:50–56. Why did God tell the Israelites to destroy the pagan altars of the people they would be conquering? Why do you suppose God reserves some of His strongest language for those who mix true religion with pagan practices? Give a modern example of such an unholy mingling.

Chapter 12: The Triumph of Good over Evil, Symbolized by a Snake

1. Imagine you are hiking down a jungle path. Suddenly you see a snake. What is your reaction? Why do you think you react this way? Why do you think Satan manifested himself to Adam and Eve as a serpent? If Satan had appeared as a more cuddly animal, such as a puppy or a kitten, would your attitude toward sin be different? What about your attitude toward snakes?

2. Read Genesis 3:14–15. What curse did God place on the serpent? What did the serpent do to deserve this curse? What good news for the world was part of Satan's curse? How would this good news be fulfilled?

3. Read Numbers 21:4–9, the story of the bronze snake. Why were so many people being bitten by snakes? Why do you think God chose the snake, rather than some other deadly creature, as His means of disciplining the Israelites? How was God's cure for snakebite redemptive in nature? How do you feel about the holy Son of God being associated with a snake, the ultimate symbol of evil? Read 2 Corinthians 5:21 and decide whether the redemption of sinners could have occurred any way other than it did: by Christ's "becoming" sin for us? Explain your answer.

4. For "the rest of the story," read 2 Kings 18:1–4. What became of the bronze snake on the pole? Mention some other religious symbols that have turned into objects of worship over time. What commandment are we breaking when we bow in adoration to an idol or revere a religious symbol? What practical steps

can we take to make sure our religious symbols do *not* become objects of worship?

PART THREE:
LESSONS TO LEARN: HOW TO HAVE
VICTORY OVER SIN, SATAN,
AND TEMPTATION

Chapter 13: Recognize Satan for Who He Is

1. Drawing on your own experience, give an example of a time when evil masqueraded as good. When and how did you become aware that you were being deceived? How did being a target of deception change the way you looked at life? How is having a healthy awareness of evil an advantage? In what ways is it a disadvantage?

2. Zero in on at least one of Satan's character traits from each of the following Scripture verses: John 8:44, John 10:10, 2 Corinthians 4:4, and 2 Corinthians 11:14. Tell how Satan uses each one of these traits to cause dissension and discord in churches. What specific actions can churches take to *"keep the unity through the bond of peace"* (Ephesians 4:3)? When is keeping unity not necessarily a wise move? What comfort can we draw from Jesus' words in Matthew 16:18?

3. Give an example of an occult practice you have either witnessed, heard of, or read about. What dangers come with involvement in the occult, even in its more "harmless" forms? How would you counsel someone who seems to be drawn to books, movies, videos or

board games that are "dark"? What Scriptures would you include in your counsel?

4. The Bible tells us to examine the things we are being taught. According to 2 Peter 1:19–21, what is the measuring rod against which all teaching is to be measured? What do theologians mean when they say the Bible is the Christian's "only rule for faith and practice?" When are other reading materials helpful? When are they potentially harmful?

Chapter 14: Take Precautions to Avoid Evil and All Appearances of It

1. In this chapter we were reminded of the importance of protecting ourselves from activities that give the "appearance of evil," as well as from activities in which evil's presence is obvious. Describe an incident in which you inadvertently gave people a wrong impression of what you were doing. What were the ramifications? Using your 20/20 hindsight, explain what you could/should have done differently.

2. When it comes to tempting situations, what advantages are there in being a Christian? In what sense are Christians more desirable targets for Satan's attacks than non-Christians? According to Psalm 119:9–16, what is one thing Christians can do ahead of time to fortify themselves against the enemy's onslaughts? Of all the temptations young people face today, which one, in your opinion, is the hardest to resist? If you had the opportunity to address a group of young people, what advice would you give?

3. Read the following Scripture passages, naming the person who sinned, the sin committed, the people affected by the sin, and the steps that could have

been taken to prevent the sin: Genesis 3:6; Genesis 9:20–25; Genesis 19; Genesis 34:2; and Joshua 7:20,21.

4. Why is it hard for Christians to stay on "the straight and narrow path"? Read Proverbs 3:5–6, restating the three instructions given. What is God's promise to those who follow these instructions? What are the advantages of having God-fearing friends?

5. Describe your decision-making process. When did you last use it, and how did it work? What changes will you make the next time you face a decision that could affect your testimony?

Chapter 15: When Tempted to Sin, Run!

1. Describe a tempting situation from which you executed a fast getaway. Which of your personal relationships would have been adversely affected if you had succumbed to the temptation and how? What, if any, financial ramifications resulted from your saying no? How do you feel about the choice you made to "run"? What Scripture verses, if any, helped you make that choice?

2. Read Genesis 39:1–23, the story of Joseph's quick exit from a tempting situation. What technique did Joseph use the first few times Potiphar's wife tried to seduce him? What reasons did he give for refusing to go to bed with her? What mistakes, if any, did Joseph make the day she caught him by the cloak? Name a possible motive behind Potiphar's wife's crying, "Rape!" How many times in this chapter does the Bible say the Lord was with Joseph? What does this repetition tell us?

3. Read 1 Corinthians10:13. What options could be included in (or excluded from) the *"way out"* God promises to provide when temptation comes? What is the wise thing to do at the following times: 1) when you sense there may be a temptation in the making, 2) when you know a temptation is upon you, 3) once the temptation has passed?

4. What role does one's conscience play in tempting situations? What makes some people heed their consciences and others ignore them? What are the causes and the results of one's conscience becoming *"seared"* (1 Timothy 4:2)? According to Hebrews 9:14, to whom should one go for a "cleansing" of the conscience?

Chapter 16: When Running Is Not an Option, Fight!

1. According to Ephesians 6:14–18, the "weapons" we Christians have at our disposal include truth, righteousness, peace, faith, salvation, the Scriptures, and prayer. Select one of these "weapons" and describe a time when you used it against the enemy. What was the outcome? What lesson(s) did you learn from this encounter?

2. Read Luke 4:1–13. What temptations did Satan use against Jesus? How did Jesus fight back? What words in the text tell us that Satan knew he had been defeated? Why would Satan decide to strike again at "an opportune time" (v 14)? What role did the Holy Spirit play in Satan's temptation of Jesus and how do you explain His involvement?

3. In John 14:6 Jesus claims, among other things, that He is *"Truth."* How do you explain the application of truth to a person (Jesus), rather than to a statement,

a book, or a concept, as is usually the case? In John 18:38 Pilate asks Jesus, *"What is truth?"* If you had been there, how would you have answered Pilate's question? How would you respond to someone who says to you, "There is no absolute truth"?

4. After reading Romans 8:28–39, what would you say is the difference between being a conqueror and being *"more than a conqueror"*? Who is mentioned as coming to our defense when we are being falsely accused? According to Romans 8:26, who else is there to defend us? What purpose might the Father have in providing not just one, but two defenders for us? When it comes to fighting Satan, is it possible to lose a few battles and still win the war? How do you know?

Chapter 17: Overcome Evil with Forgiveness and Love

1. Who is hurt more by the desire to get even: the one with the vengeful heart or the one targeted for the revenge? Why? Describe a time when someone you know retaliated against someone who hurt him/her. What happened as a result of the retaliation? In light of the advice given in Romans 12:17–21, what should be the behavior of Christians who have been wronged? How does this behavior grant the wronged one victory?

2. According to Matthew 6:15, there is a price to pay when we fail to forgive. What is it? Does this warning mean that God's forgiveness of us is dependent on our forgiveness of others, or does it mean that those of us who have been forgiven by God will, by virtue of our "new natures," want to forgive those who *"trespass against us"*? Explain your answer. In

your opinion, who benefits the most: the bestower of forgiveness or the recipient? Why?

3. How would you counsel someone who says, "I just can't forgive him"? What Scripture verses would you use? Why is God's grace a necessary ingredient in the act of forgiveness? What could happen if God is left out of the forgiveness process?

4. According to Matthew 5:23,24 and Luke 17:3,4, what specific action is the Christian required to take in order to mend a broken relationship? If everything that God requires has been done and a broken relationship has not been restored, is it possible for the one who tried to make amends to experience *"the joy of the Lord?"* Why or why not? Take a moment to pray about an unresolved relationship with which you are currently struggling.

Chapter 18: Learn to Live in Christ's Victory

1. In times of persecution, what causes some people to turn away from God and others to embrace God more fully? What, if anything, can Christians do to prepare for persecution? Name some blessings that come with persecution.

2. In what ways does persecution effect in us a closer identification with the Savior, specifically with His humiliation, His sufferings, His death, His burial, His resurrection, His ascension, His ministry of intercession, and His eventual triumph over evil?

3. When you think about the future, how do you feel: certain or uncertain, encouraged or discouraged, optimistic or pessimistic? Why? Give some examples

of Western society's attempts to reverse the effects of aging and to deny the horrors of death. According to 2 Corinthians 4:16–18, what is God's compensation for the ravages of the aging process, and what can older (and younger) people do to live in victory? How should God's view of death, given in Psalm 116:15, affect the believer's view of death?

4. Read 2 Corinthians 5:1–10. When the apostle Paul thinks about leaving his *"earthly tent"* (body), how does he feel? What brings him comfort? What does Paul say should be our most important goal in life (v 9)? Name one thing you would like to change in your life in order to achieve this goal.

5. What insights did you gain from this study on evil as it relates to God, to Satan, to yourself, to the church, to the world, to the future, etc? If you could ask God one question right now, what would it be? Take a moment to thank the Lord that He is sovereign over all things.

ENDNOTES

[1] Quoted by R. C. Sproul, Jr. "Unto the Lord," *Tabletalk*, October 2002, p.2.

[2] Richard Gamble, "Without Fear," *Tabletalk*, May 2002, p.10.

[3] Rick Warren, *The Purpose Driven Life* (Grand Raids, MI, Zondervan Publishing House, 2002), p.194.

[4] *Favorites for Youth* (Gospel Songs and Choruses), Singspiration Music (Zondervan), Grand Rapids, Mi, 1975, p.102.

[5] Jennifer L. Bayne and Sarah E. Hinlicky, "Free to Be Creatures Again." *Christianity Today*, October 23, 2000, p.41.

[6] *Westminster Confession of Faith*, III, 1–2.

[7] From an interview with journalist Cal Thomas, reported by Tony Carnes, "Conservative like a Fox," *Christianity Today*, July 2004, p.54.

244 · MAKING SENSE OF EVIL

[8] William Edgar, "Ain't It Hard? Suffering and Hope in the Blues." *Modern Reformation*, January/February 2005, p.36.

[9] From *Matthew Henry's Concise Commentary on the Whole Bible* (Nashville, TN: Thomas Nelson Publishers, 1997), p.166.

[10] Quoted by Robert Wernech, "Who the Devil is the Devil?" *Smithsonian*, October 1999, p.23.

Printed in the United States
76375LV00002B/1-99